KUBO POWER

Quick and Simple Steps to Mastering the Kubotan Keychain

SAMMY FRANCO

C000004624

Kubotan Power

Also by Sammy Franco

The Complete Body Opponent Bag Book
Heavy Bag Training: Boxing, Mixed Martial Arts & Self-Defense
Gun Safety: For Home Defense and Concealed Carry
Out of the Cage: A Complete Guide to Beating a Mixed Martial Artist on the Street
Warrior Wisdom: Inspiring Ideas from the World's Greatest Warriors
Judge, Jury and Executioner
Savage Street Fighting: Tactical Savagery as a Last Resort
Feral Fighting: Level 2 WidowMaker
War Craft: Street Fighting Tactics of the War Machine
War Machine: How to Transform Yourself Into a Vicious and Deadly Street Fighter
The Bigger They Are, The Harder They Fall: How to Defeat a Larger & Stronger Adversary in a Street Fight
First Strike: Mastering the Preemptive Strike for Street Combat
1001 Street Fighting Secrets: The Principles of Contemporary Fighting Arts
When Seconds Count: Everyone's Guide to Self-Defense
Killer Instinct: Unarmed Combat for Street Survival
Street Lethal: Unarmed Urban Combat

Kubotan Power
Copyright © 2014 by Sammy Franco
ISBN 978-0-9853472-6-0
Printed in the United States of America

Published by Contemporary Fighting Arts, LLC.
P.O. Box 84028
Gaithersburg, Maryland 20883 USA
Phone: (301) 279-2244
Visit us Online at: www.sammyfranco.com

For author interviews or publicity information, please send inquiries in care of the publisher.

ii

Table of Contents

Preface

The Kubotan is an incredible self-defense weapon that has helped thousands of people effectively defend themselves. Men, women, law enforcement officers, military, and security professionals alike, appreciate this small and discreet self-defense tool.

Unfortunately, however, very little has been written about the kubotan, leaving it shrouded by both mystery and ignorance. As a result, most people don't know how to unleash the full power of this unique personal defense weapon

Well, all of this is about to change. With over 290 photographs and step-by-step instructions, ***Kubotan Power: Quick and Simple Steps to Mastering the Kubotan Keychain*** is the authoritative resource for mastering this devastating weapon.

Kubotan Power leaves no stone unturned by providing seven chapters covering these essential topics: how to choose the right kubotan, tactical flashlight conversions, combat applications, grips, tactical do's and don'ts, weapon nomenclature, impact shock, self-defense stages, high and low concealment positions, weapon deployment, target awareness, vital targets and medical implications, use of force considerations, attributes of fighting, defensive techniques, takedowns, training and flow drills, ground fighting, and much more.

Best of all, the skills and techniques featured in this book can also be applied to other ubiquitous items such as the tactical flashlight, mini mag light, tactical pen, and yawara mini stick.

Kubotan Power should be treated as a skill building workbook. So please feel free to write in the margins, underline passages, and dog ear the pages. Also, I strongly encourage you to read this book from beginning to end, chapter by chapter. Only after you have read the entire book should you treat it like a reference and skip around to subjects that pique your interest.

Finally, at the end of this book I have included a glossary of terms for your convenience.

I wish you all the best of luck in your training.

Sammy Franco
Founder & President
Contemporary Fighting Arts

Important!

The information and techniques in this book can be dangerous and could lead to serious injury. The author, publisher, and distributors of this book disclaim any liability from loss, injury, or damage, personal or otherwise, resulting from the information and procedures in this book. This book is for academic study only.

It is the reader's responsibility to research and comply with all local, state and federal laws and regulations pertaining to the possession, carry, and use of a kubotan.

Chapter One
The Kubotan

The Kubotan is a close-quarter self-defense weapon that can be used as both an impact tool and pain compliance device. This sturdy mini stick is approximately the size of a thick magic marker and it often has a keyring attached to its end.

The kubotan can be made out of a wide range of different materials, including steel, aluminum, wood and unbreakable plastic. However, the most destructive types are made of solid steel.

Unlike other self-defense weapons, the kubotan is discreet and looks innocuous. To many people it's nothing more than a nondescript keychain and therefore can be transported and concealed very easily. Best of all, the kubotan is inexpensive and can be easily purchased.

The kubotan comes in a variety of colors and designs. Pictured here, two pointed aluminum kubotans.

Why Carry a Kubotan?

There are a number of advantages to using a kubotan in a self-defense situation. First, a kubotan functions as a highly effective impact tool. It permits the average person to effectively defend themselves by delivering devastating blows that far exceed a typical punch. This is particularly important to people who are too small or weak to deliver fisted blows.

With proper training, the kubotan can also function as both a pain compliance and leverage tool when applying joint locks or submission holds.

From a use-of-force perspective, the kubotan is versatile. Unlike a firearm and knife, the kubotan can be used as an effective intermediate use of force weapon that can be applied in a wide variety of fighting environments. However, it can also be used during the most dire self-defense circumstances where lethal force is warrant and justify in the eyes of the law.

There are many other reasons why you should consider carrying a kubotan for self-defense, here are a few more:

- It's lightweight.
- It's inconspicuous.
- It's small and can be used as an everyday carry (EDC) item.
- It doesn't require reloading.
- It won't jam or misfire.
- It can be used as a pain compliance tool.
- It can be used as an impact weapon.
- It can be used as both a lethal and non lethal weapon.
- It permits smaller or weaker people to generate tremendous striking power.
- Kubotan techniques can be applied to ubiquitous items such as mini flashlights, tactical pens, yawara palm sticks, etc.

Although some people prefer the spiked kubotan, it's not recommended for real world self-defense applications.

Important: *Regardless of your reasons for carrying a kubotan, remember it's your sole responsibility to research and comply with all local, state and federal laws and regulations pertaining to the possession, carry, and use of a kubotan.*

Choosing The Right Kubotan

There are a wide variety of kubotans on the market, some are good and some bad. Real bad! For example, the spiked kubotan is popular and sold by the thousands, however it's still a very poor choice for real world self-defense applications.

First, the spikes restrict your ability to use certain hand grips (more will be discussed in the chapter three). Essentially, the spiked kubotan will only permit you to use the "center point grip."

Second, if you decide to deliver a punch (called fist loading) with this type of kubotan, the spikes will significantly reduce the power of your strike. In the best case scenario, you end up poking two small holes in the attacker's face, causing him to be further enraged.

Third, the spikes turn the kubotan's innocuous and nondescript characteristics into a menacing looking weapon. From a legal perspective, this can be problematic for you. Imagine having to explain why you were carrying such a "dangerous looking" weapon to a police officer, judge or jury.

With so many different types of kubotans on the market, it can be a bit overwhelming when trying to buy one. Does it matter if it's made of plastic or metal? Does it need to have a keyring attached to it? Should I buy one that has a sharp point at its end? What is the ideal kubotan for self-defense?

What follows, is a list of important characteristics you should keep in mind when buying a kubotan.

Essential Kubotan Characteristics

- **Minimum Weight of 7 ounces**
- **Minimum Length of 5.5 inches**
- **Dark or Muted Color**
- **Keyring Attachment**
- **Innocuous Looking**
- **Flat Ends**

Weight Requirement

For a kubotan to be an effective striking weapon, it must have a bit of weight. For all intent and purposes, it should have a minimum weight of approximately seven ounces. This weight is important for one simple reason - striking power!

When a kubotan has this amount of appreciable weight, it will magnify the impact of the actual strike. This is especially important if you are going to use "fist loading" techniques. I'll discuss fist loading techniques later in this book.

Pictured here, a lightweight aluminum kubotan with a flat end.

The unfortunate fact is most commercial kubotans are made of lightweight aluminum that weighs approximately two or three ounces. Most people like this lightweight feature because it makes the kubotan less cumbersome, especially when it's used as an everyday carry item (EDC).

However, this lightweight feature is not ideal for self-defense purposes. The bottom line is, you need the extra weight if you want the kubotan to be an effective self-defense weapon.

Frankly, it all boils down to priorities. If you are using a kubotan as a simple keychain, then it doesn't really matter how much it weighs. Just attach your keys to it and you are done!

However, if you are carrying a kubotan for self-defense purposes, then you owe it to yourself to carry one that is hefty enough to effectively incapacitate a vicious criminal attacker. So, make certain it weighs a minimum of seven ounces.

Length Requirement

The next requirement is length. Make certain your kubotan has a minimum length of 5.5 inches. This should not be much of a problem considering most commercial kubotans will almost always measure approximately 5.5 inches long. This length requirement is important to accommodate large hands and for implementing leveraging techniques.

Dark or Muted Color

Purchase a kubotan that is dark or muted in color. Black is preferred. This is important when defending against an attacker in dark or low light conditions.

Avoid using a bright or shiny kubotan. For example, you don't want light to shine off your kubotan when attempting to conceal it from your adversary.

Believe it or not, the keyring is an important component of the kubotan.

Keyring Attachment

The keyring attachment is important for two reasons. First, it converts this self-defense weapon into a practical keychain allowing you to carry it with you at all times.

Second, it makes the kubotan look less threatening. Remember, your kubotan should appear innocuous. This is especially important if your self-defense situation turns into a legal battle.

Innocuous Looking

As I stated earlier, a kubotan should look harmless to the layperson. The last thing you want to do is bring attention to your weapon. Avoid carrying a kubotan that has spikes, sharp points or any type of designs that look threatening or menacing.

Also, just because a kubotan doesn't look menacing doesn't guarantee that you won't be stopped by the police. As a matter of fact, the TSA classifies the kubotan as a "martial arts & self-defense item" and prohibits it as a carry on item. So, remember to check it in when flying.

Avoid carrying a kubotan that looks dangerous or threatening. Pictured here, a pointed kubotan that looks menacing.

Pictured here, custom made steel kubotans.

Flat Ends

The kubotan should have a two flat ends. Avoid carrying one with a pointed tip. Remember, the kubotan is an "impact weapon" and pain compliance tool, not a cutting or puncturing device.

When used correctly, the kubotan it designed to break bones and damage soft tissue. Puncturing the assailant's skin with a pointed tip will certinly not incapacitate a well seasoned criminal attacker.

The mini Koga made by Cold Steel has a solid design, but it falls short as a impact weapon because of its pointed tips.

The Koga SD made by Cold Steel is a solid impact weapon and a much better alternative to its cousin, the mini Koga. Notice its flat ends.

Kubotan Nomenclature

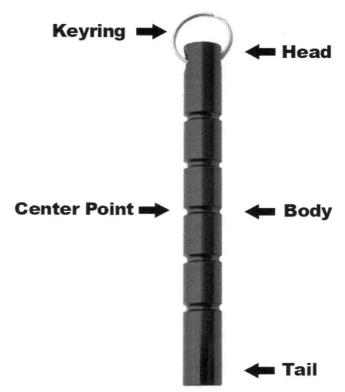

Like any self-defense weapon, take the time to become familiar with the kubotan's nomenclature.

Tactical Flashlights and Pens

There might be circumstances that prohibit you from owning or carrying a kubotan. In such a situation, you can replace it with other ubiquitous items, such as a tactical flashlight or tactical pen. Just be certain that the item you choose meets the same requirements discussed earlier.

If you have a choice between a tactical flashlight or pen, go with a flashlight. Actually, I strongly encourage you to avoid using a tactical pen as a replacement for the kubotan.

The main problem with tactical pens is they have sharp points. This means they cannot function as an impact weapon and can only be used as a puncturing tool. While a puncturing tool can be effective under certain circumstances, it's limited in scope. Especially, in self-defense situations that don't warrant the application of lethal force.

The tactical flashlight, on the other hand, is a great alternative to the kubotan. And in some cases, is superior to the kubotan. That's right! It's better. Let me explain why.

First, the tactical flashlight is an illumination tool that allows you to see in the dark or during low light conditions. Second, a good tactical flashlight can temporarily blind and disorient your attacker, allowing you to either strike or escape to safety. Third, you can perform the very same techniques with a tactical flashlight that you can with a kubotan.

Finally, the tactical flashlight is one of the most discreet looking weapon on the planet, making it less menacing looking than any kubotan on the market.

Choosing a tactical flashlight to replace a kubotan will boil down to personal preference. However, here are a few requirements to keep in mind when choosing one specifically for self-defense applications.

Tactical Flashlight Requirements

If you are considering replacing a kubotan with a tactical flashlight, be certain it meets some of the following requirements:

- The more powerful the bulb the better, just be certain it's impact resistant.

- The flashlight's construction must be solid, allowing you to use it effectively as an impact weapon.

- The ergonomics of the flashlight should permit you to hold it comfortably using any type of kubotan grip.

- The flashlight's construction and materials should provide a sturdy grip to help minimize impact shock.

- When held in its center, the flashlight should protrude at least 3/4 of an inch on each end of your fist.

- The flashlight should weigh a minimum of seven ounces.

- It should be dark or muted in color.

- It should have a clip or carrier system that permits instant access and rapid deployment.

- It should have a pushbutton tail cap.

The SureFire E2D LED Defender Ultra Flashlight.

Surefire makes some of the best illumination tools in the world. Pictured here, the P2X Fury Defender.

Nitecore MT21A tactical flashlight.

Nitecore MH2c tactical flashlight.

Fenix LD22 tactical flashlight.

Fenix LD20 tactical flashlight.

Pictured here, the Pocket Shark magic marker made by Cold Steel.

The Smith & Wesson tactical pen and stylus is not a suitable replacement for a kubotan.

Kubotan Power

Chapter Two
Applications

Most people assume the kubotan is simply an impact weapon. In reality, this unique self-defense device can perform many other self-defense applications.

As a matter of fact, there are a broad range of effective self-defense techniques that can be used with just a minimal amount of training.

In my Contemporary Fighting Arts self-defense system, I have classified the kubotan's applications into five unique categories. They include the following:

- **Pain Compliance Tool**
- **Anchoring Tool**
- **Striking Tool**
- **Fist Loading Tool**
- **Razing Tool**

Pain Compliance Tool

Not every self-defense situation is going to be the same. As a matter of fact, there might be situations or circumstances where you are legally and morally required to control or subdue your attacker.

For example, if you were a police officer, security guard or hospital employee required to control and gain compliance from an emotionally disturbed person (EDP).

Fortunately, the kubotan permits you to gain compliance from your adversary by controlling sensitive pressure points of the body. More will be discussed in chapter six.

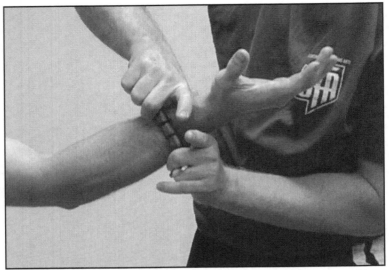

The kubotan makes an ideal pain compliance tool. Pictured here, a practitioner applies a wrist control technique.

Anchoring Tool

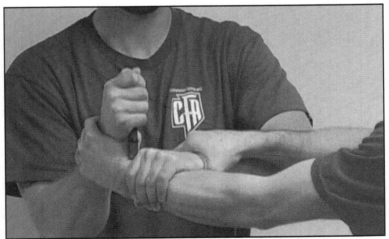

You can counter many wrist grabs with the kubotan. In this photo, the practitioner on the left counters a two-hand wrist grab with a pain compliance technique.

The kubotan can also function as an anchoring tool. Essentially, "anchoring" is used for two purposes.

First, anchoring allows you to trap, pin or isolate the assailant's limb in place. It functions as a temporary control technique, allowing you to either strike him with your free hand or safely transition to a more advantageous position.

Second, anchoring allows you to solidify submission holds on your adversary. With anchoring, you can actually apply a wide variety of grappling and ground fighting techniques with the kubotan placed in your hand.

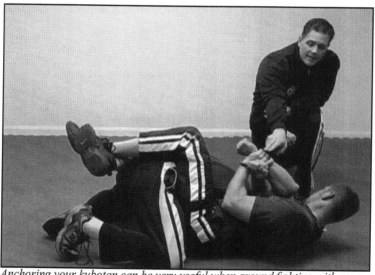

Anchoring your kubotan can be very useful when ground fighting with your adversary. In this photo, a shoulder crank technique is applied from the leg guard position. Notice how the kubotan functions as an anchor, allowing the defender to solidify a submission hold.

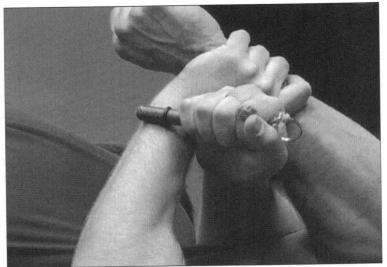

A close-up of the anchoring technique.

In this photo, the practitioner uses the anchoring technique to perform a submission hold from the top mounted position.

Striking Tool

The kubotan shows its real power when used as a striking tool. As a matter of fact, the amount of force that is generated from a kubotan strike is truly amazing.

When used properly, a kubotan strike on a vital anatomical target can bring the most aggressive adversary to his knees in agony.

However, you must know how and where to strike these vital targets. Some include: the eyes, temple, throat, back of neck, spine, etc. I'll discuss these vital targets in a later chapter.

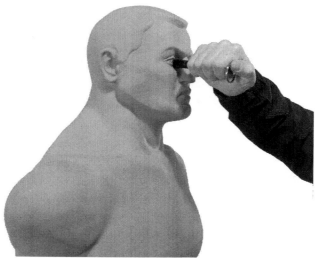

The kubotan can be a devastating striking tool. However, be certain you know how and where to strike the opponent. Pictured here, the author practices eye strikes on the body opponent bag.

Fist Loading Tool

One of the hidden benefits of the kubotan is "fist loading." Essentially, fist loading is the process of delivering fisted blows with kubotan in your hand. The added weight of the kubotan in your hand significantly increases the power of a conventional punches. The fist loading concept is very similar to punching someone with a roll of nickels in your hand.

Kubotan Power

Once again, fist loading will only work if your kubotan has a minimum weight of seven ounces. This is why I instruct my students to use steel kubotans instead of aluminum. Believe me, the extra ounces are worth its weight in gold!

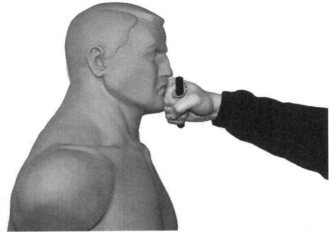

Fist loading is just one advantage of using a kubotan. In this photo, the author delivers a lead straight punch with the kubotan in his hand.

Pictured here, a student develops his fist loading techniques on the punching mitts.

Razing Tool

The kubotan can also be used when "razing" the adversary. Razing is a unique combat methodology found in my Widow Maker Program. This vicious fighting style was specifically designed to provide law-abiding citizens with lethal force techniques when faced with the immediate threat of an unlawful deadly criminal attack.

Basically, razing involves a series of vicious close-quarter techniques designed to physically and psychologically incapacitate a criminal attacker.

These close-quarter techniques are executed at various beats (half beat, quarter beat and zero beat) and they include: eye raking, gouging, tearing, crushing, biting, hair pulling, elbow strikes, head butts, bicep pops, neck cranks, shaving forearms, and finishing chokes.

Unfortunately, it would take an entire book to adequately teach you the Widow Maker methodology, however the point I want to make is the kubotan can also be used as a supplemental razing tool.

In the following photo sequence, the author demonstrates some of the razing techniques that can be applied in close-quarter combat. Keep in mind, the kubotan can be used in conjunction with this unconventional fighting style.

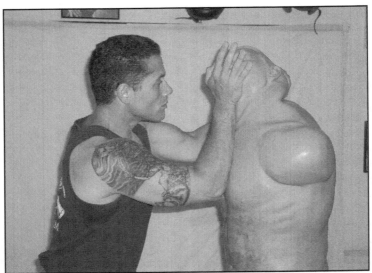

Applying the neck crank technique.

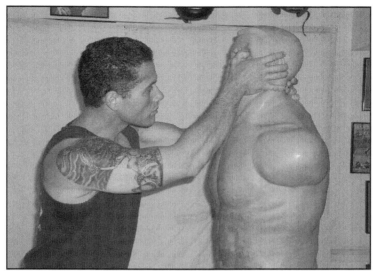

Applying the thumb gouge technique.

Applying the shaving forearm technique.

Applying elbow strikes.

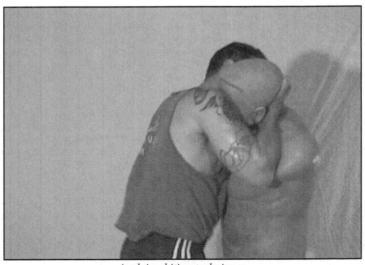

Applying biting techniques.

Chapter Three
Grips

In order to effectively use the kubotan, you need a basic understanding of grips. Actually, kubotan grips are vital because they determine which anatomical targets you can strike and which techniques you can apply.

For example, if you were holding the kubotan with a hammer grip, it would be awkward to strike the adversary in his eyes. The grip ergonomics place too much pressure on your wrists when trying to strike this target. Instead, a more appropriate striking target would be the assailant's elbows.

There are six kubotan grips that you should be familiar with and they include:

- **Hammer**
- **Ice pick**
- **Modified ice pick**
- **Reinforced ice pick**
- **Center point**
- **Saber**

Hammer Grip

The hammer grip is the exact type of grip you would use if you were holding an actual hammer. Hence, the name - hammer grip.

Generally, when performing the hammer grip, the exposed area of the kubotan will be seen above your thumb line.

The hammer grip is often used to deliver upward strikes to targets such the groin, elbows, chin, and throat.

The hammer grip.

Ice Pick Grip

Next, is the ice pick grip. As you can imagine, this grip is similar to holding an ice pick in your hand. Generally, the exposed area of the kubotan will be seen below your pinky. The ice pick grip is often used to deliver downward strikes to targets such as the eyes, nose, collarbone, throat, back of neck, spine, ribs, and hands.

The ice pick grip.

Modified Ice Pick Grip

Of all the kubotan grips, the modified ice pick grip is the most important one to master.

To apply this grip, you would hold the kubotan in the ice pick grip with your thumb placed firmly on top of the weapon. Once again, the exposed area of the kubotan will be seen below your pinky.

The thumb positioning on the modified ice pick grip is especially important. It helps reinforce your grip, allowing you to deliver full-force strikes without dislodging the weapon from your hand. As a matter of fact, the modified ice pick is the only grip that permits you to safely hit the adversary with full-power striking techniques. Targets include: the eyes, nose, collarbone, throat, back of neck, spine, ribs, and hands.

The modified ice pick grip.

27

Reinforced Ice Pick Grip

The reinforced ice pick grip is primarily used to drive the kubotan into sensitive pressure point targets.

To apply this grip, hold the kubotan like an ice pick with the palm of your free hand placed on top of the weapon. The exposed area of the kubotan will be seen below your pinky.

The reinforced ice pick grip.

Center Point Grip

The center point grip is used for fist loading techniques. To perform the grip, grasp the center of the kubotan so the exposed area of the weapon will be seen equally above the thumb and below your pinky.

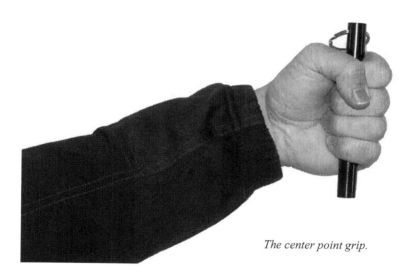

The center point grip.

Saber Grip

With the saber grip, you would hold the kubotan in the same way that you would hold a saber sword, with the thumb extended forward. The exposed area of the kubotan is visible above your thumb line.

The saber grip is generally used for delivering linear thrusts to selected soft tissue targets like the eyes and throat.

The saber grip.

Grip Orientation Drill

Now, it's time to become familiar with these kubotan grips so they become second nature and can be readily applied under the duress of a self-defense altercation.

Here, is a grip orientation drill that will help you master the different kubotan grips.

1. Begin with the kubotan in your right hand.

2. Next, have a friend, spouse or training partner call out various kubotan grips.

3. Quickly configure the different kubotan grips at the pace of the commands.

4. Perform this exercise for five minutes.

5. Switch hands and begin again for another five minutes.

Once you have this drill down, have your partner increase the cadence of the verbal commands while you perform the exercise with your eyes closed.

Don't Flail The Kubotan!

Since kubotans are used as everyday keychains, the key portion is often used as a flailing weapon to whip across an attacker's face. While this may sound like a solid self-defense technique to some people, avoid doing it!

Failing your keys into your assailant's eyes is one of the worst things you can do. Actually, it's a worthless move that will simply enrage your attacker and most likely provoke greater violence.

Remember, the kubotan is a target specific self-defense weapon that must be deliberately applied to a specific anatomical target with appreciable force. For example, if your objective is to attack the assailant's eyes, you will yield much better results if you strike him directly in the eye with the tail of the weapon.

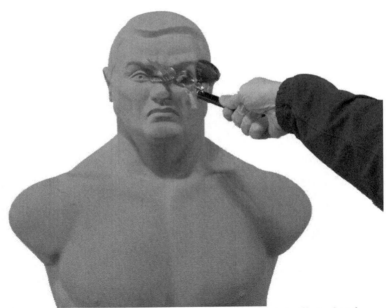

Whipping or flailing your keys across the attacker's face is ineffectual and should be avoided in a self-defense situation.

Impact Shock

Now that you are familiar with the different types of kubotan grips, it's important to make certain that you can maintain the structural integrity of your grip and retain your weapon when striking your adversary.

Unfortunately, I see too many self-defense instructors placing too much emphasis on striking with the kubotan and not enough on retention skills.

When I say "retention", I mean holding on to the weapon when delivering a powerful strike or applying a pressure point hold. Remember, the best targets for striking are sensitive bony targets that are closest to the surface of the skin.

Well, this means that each and every time you strike a target, you run the risk of dislodging the weapon from your hand. It's just a fact that you have to accept. It's the price of doing business in the streets.

Unfortunately, many untrained people have actually dislodged and dropped their kubotan during a self-defense altercation because they never anticipated the "impact shock" of the target.

Impact shock is the resistance your hand and arm receives when the kubotan makes contact with a hard or resistant surface. If you want to maintain your grip and hold on to your weapon, you must anticipate this and train for it.

One of the best ways to prepare yourself for impact shock, is to regularly practice striking hard surfaces with your kubotan.

Unfortunately, the Body Opponent Bag or BOB won't work because its material is too soft and doesn't provide the necessary resistance to truly test the structural integrity of your grip.

Don't get me wrong, the Body Opponent Bag is great for kubotan training (more is discussed in a later chapter) but not for impact shock training.

Therefore, you will need to find something that provides significant resistance. The best material is wood. Perhaps, a dead tree in your backyard or an old piece of lumber lying in your garage.

A word of caution, don't strike any hard surfaces with full-force until your grip, hands and arms are first acclimated to the power. My suggestion is to start off with twenty-five percent of your power and progressively increase it over time. Practice this with all six of the kubotan grips.

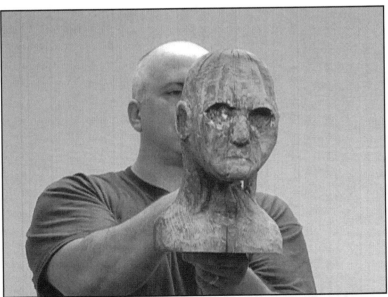

Pictured here, a custom-made striking target designed specifically for impact shock. It's called the "Bullick" and it's made of locust wood. Locust wood is extremely hard and durable and will thoroughly test the structural integrity of any kubotan grip.

Practicing throat strikes.

Practicing eye strikes.

Kubotan Power

Chapter Four
Concealment Positions

Before learning how to conceal the kubotan, it's important to first discuss the two stages of self-defense and how they relate to kubotan stances and strategic postures. Essentially, the two stages of self-defense are:

- **Pre-Contact Stage**
- **Contact Stage**

The Pre-Contact Stage of Self-Defense

The pre-contact stage of self-defense refers to the seconds or moments prior to physically engaging with your assailant. During the pre-contact stage, you are either aware or unaware of the threat that awaits you.

The Aware State

During the aware state of the pre-contact stage, you actually have time to prepare yourself both mentally and physically for violence.

In some cases, you might actually have the opportunity to engage in dialogue with your adversary before it leads to violence.

Say, for example, you are enjoying the night out with a few friends at a local bar. It's noisy and crowded and you happen to accidentally spill your beer on a slightly inebriated patron. As you can imagine, he immediately becomes enraged and begins to threaten you. You are experiencing an aware state of a pre-contact self-defense situation, requiring you to (hopefully) defuse the hostile person.

The Unaware State

During the unaware state of the pre-contact stage, you don't have time to prepare yourself mentally and physically for violence. In the

During the aware state of the pre-contact stage, you actually have time to prepare yourself both mentally and physically for violence.

preceding moments before an attack, you're unaware of your adversary's presence or intentions. Essentially, you are caught off guard and never see the danger coming.

The best way to avoid being taken by surprise is to try and work on your situational awareness skills. Situational awareness is total alertness, presence, and focus on virtually everything in your immediate surroundings.

Pictured here, an unaware state of the pre-contact stage of self-defense. The two women on the left are unaware of what is waiting for them around the corner.

With practice, you can train your senses to detect and assess the people, places, objects, and actions that can pose a danger to you and your loved ones. Do not think of situational awareness simply in terms of the five customary senses of sight, sound, smell, taste, and touch. In addition, the very real powers of instinct and intuition must also be developed and eventually relied upon.

Two vagrants congregating on the street corner or by your car, the stranger lingering at the mailboxes in your lobby, the delivery man at the door, a deserted parking lot, an alleyway near a familiar sidewalk, the stray dog ambling toward you in the park, a large limb hanging precariously from a tree . . . these are all obvious examples of persons, places, and objects that pose a threat to you. Situational awareness need not - and should not - be limited to preconceived notions about obvious sources of danger.

Situational awareness is one of the cornerstones of common sense self-defense. How would you rate this woman's state of awareness?

Situational awareness is total alertness, presence, and focus on virtually every-thing in your immediate surroundings.

The Contact Stage of Self-Defense

In the contact stage of self-defense, you are actually physically fighting or defending against your assailant.

For example, while attempting to deescalate a drunk at the bar, he cocks his arm back and takes a swing at your head. In response, you block his attack and gain control over the man.

Another example is, you're on your way home from work and happen to walk past a dark alley. As you turn the corner, a large figure jumps you from behind. Before you have time to react, the assailant grabs and places you in a rear bear hug, pinning both of your arms to your sides.

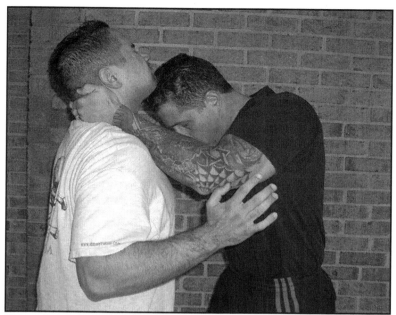

Pictured here, the author demonstrates a ramming head butt strike during the contact stage of self-defense.

The Kubotan and the Self-Defense Stages

I have some good news for you! The kubotan can be used effectively in both the pre-contact and contact stages of self-defense. Let's first talk about using it in the pre-contact stage.

Pre-Contact Applications

Effectively using the kubotan during the pre-contact stages will require you to conceal the weapon from your potential adversary. That's right! You have to hide it from him. This is important for the following two reasons:

- **Escalation Prevention** - As I mentioned earlier, in the pre-contact stage, there might be an opportunity to deescalate or diffuse a hostile person from using violence. In such a scenario, you want the kubotan ready, but you don't want to alert your adversary of its presence. Doing so would only escalate his anger.

- **Element of Surprise** - There's an old saying, "The hardest punch, is the one you never see coming." The same adage applies to the kubotan. If possible, don't let the adversary know you have a weapon. You want the element of surprise if and when your decide to fight back.

Regardless of your intended objective, in order to effectively conceal the kubotan during the pre-contact stages of self-defense, you must master two strategic stances: the high and low concealment positions.

The High Concealment Position

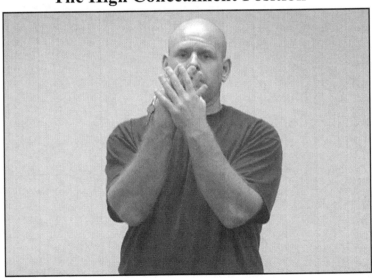

The first stance I'm going to teach you is the high concealment position and it's only used when you are faced with a pre-contact self-defense situation.

This stance is best used when you are faced with a threatening opponent at close proximity and you have the time and opportunity to assume a strategic posture with the kubotan concealed in your hands.

The high concealment position is ideal because it provides you with the following benefits:

- **Kubotan concealment**
- **Speed of deployment**
- **Striking power**
- **Mobility**
- **Balance and Stability**
- **Offensive fluidity**
- **Maximizes kubotan reach**

The key to this deceptive stance is the centerline. The centerline is an imaginary vertical line that divides your body in half. Located on this line are some of your vital targets (i.e., eyes, nose, chin, throat, solar plexus, and groin).

When confronted by a threatening adversary, it's important to position your centerline approximately forty-five degrees from the opponent. This will help protect your vital targets and help provide stability to your stance.

To assume the high concealment stance, stand with both of your legs approximately shoulder width apart. Position your body at a forty-five degree angle from the adversary. Keep your knees bent, both hands up, and fifty percent of your weight on each leg. And remember to keep your neck, shoulders, and arms relaxed.

Next, keep both of your hands up with your palms facing you. Use your thumb to keep the kubotan tucked into your hand. This hand positioning will effectively conceal the kubotan behind your palms and forearms. Remember, concealing the kubotan in this fashion will provide you with the element of surprise, if you have to deploy the weapon.

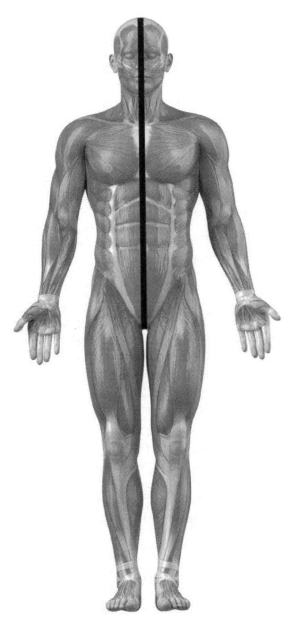

The centerline plays an important role with strategic stances.

When using the high concealment position, remember to use your thumb to keep the kubotan tucked in your hand.

Pictured here, the high concealment position. Can you see the kubotan?

A bird's eye view of the high concealment position.

A side view of the high concealment position.

The high concealment position should appear natural and nonthreatening to the adversary.

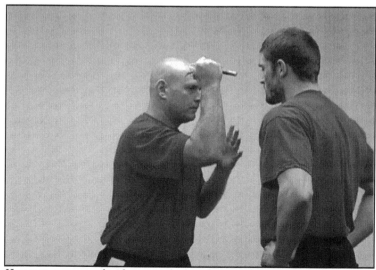

However, once you decide to attack, the adversary has very little time to react.

The Low Concealment Position

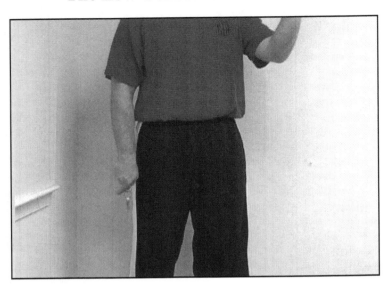

Next, is the low concealment position and it's generally used for the following purposes:

- To conceal the kubotan when walking in public places.
- As a transition to the high concealment position.

Here's an example of the low concealment position in action. Let's say, you are walking to your car with your kubotan held in a low concealment position. As you make your way through the parking lot, you are suddenly approached by a threatening adversary.

In such a situation, you maintain the low concealment position so long as your adversary keeps his distance from you. In the event he steps closer, you would transition to the more advantageous high concealment position.

The low concealment position should only be used when the adversary is a good distance away from you such as the neutral zone or kicking range of unarmed combat.

Avoid using the low concealment position in the punching or

grappling ranges of unarmed combat. Doing so can make you vulnerable to an attack. Remember, you must always have both hands up when confronted at close distances.

Assuming the Low Concealment Position

Like the high concealment posture, the low concealment position also requires you to conceal the kubotan behind your palm and forearm. The only difference is you are holding the kubotan by your thigh and with only one hand.

To assume the low concealment position, keep your legs approximately shoulder width apart. Angle your body approximately forty-five degrees from your adversary with both of your knees slightly bent. Keep fifty percent of your weight distributed over each leg and remain relaxed and prepared.

Next, let your kubotan hand relax against the side of your leg with the weapon being concealed by your palm and forearm. If time permits, keep your free hand up.

Pictured here, the practitioner of the right uses the kubotan low concealment position in the neutral zone.

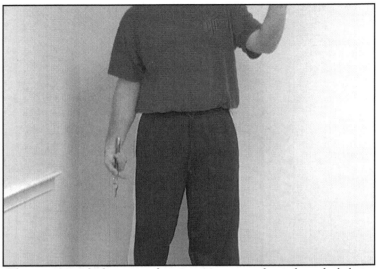

When assuming the low concealment position, remember to keep the kubotan pressed firmly against the inside of your wrist and forearm.

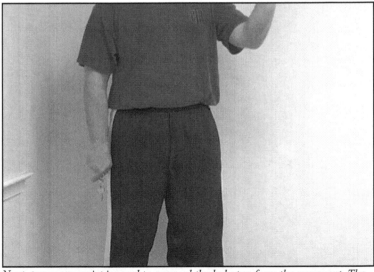

Next, turn your wrist inward to conceal the kubotan from the opponent. The only visible object should be your keys.

A close-up photo of the low concealment position. Notice how the kubotan is hidden behind the wrist and forearm.

The following scenario demonstrates how you can transition from a low to high concealment position. We begin with the defender (left) casually walking in a low concealment position.

The assailant (right) surprises the defender with a chest push.

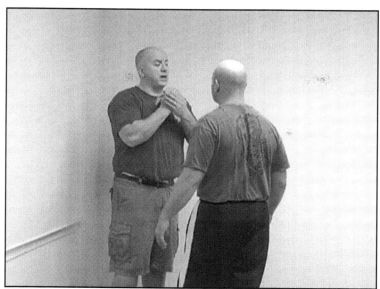

Without showing his kubotan to the adversary, the defender raises both of his arms into a high concealment position.

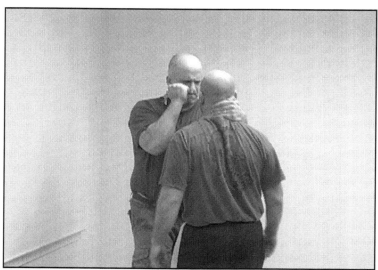

The defender is now able to defend himself.

Kubotan Power

Chapter Five
Offensive Techniques

Defending yourself with a kubotan requires you to possess a variety of fighting attributes. Essentially, attributes are mental and physical qualities that enhance combat skills and techniques. Some attributes include: power, speed, accuracy, timing, and balance.

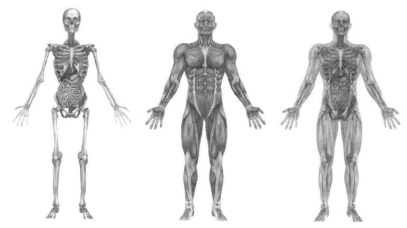

However, one of the most important attributes for the kubotan is target awareness. Simply put, target awareness is a culmination of five interdependent principles. They are:

- **Target orientation**
- **Target recognition**
- **Target selection**
- **Target impaction**
- **Target exploitation**

Let's first take a look at target orientation and see how it directly relates to the kubotan.

Target Orientation

Target orientation means having a workable knowledge of specific anatomical targets that are especially vulnerable to the kubotan. These targets can be found in one of three possible target zones.

Target Zones

Zone 1 (head region) - consists of targets related to the assailant's senses, including the eyes, temples, nose, chin, and back of neck.

Zone 2 (neck, torso, and groin) - consists of targets related to the assailant's breathing, including the throat, solar plexus, ribs, and groin.

Zone 3 (legs and feet) - consists of anatomical targets related to the assailant's mobility, including the thighs, knees, shins, and instep/toes.

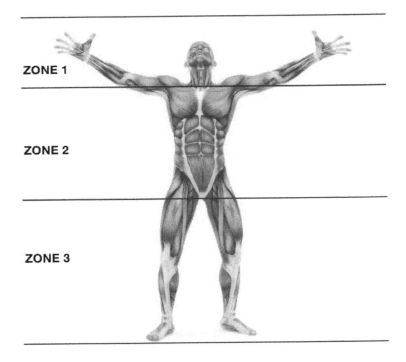

Simply knowing the specific locations of various anatomical targets is not enough. Target orientation also requires that you have a strong understanding of the medical implications of striking these targets.

As a matter of fact, if you intend on using a kubotan for self-defense purposes you have a moral and legal responsibility to know the medical implications of each and every offensive strike and technique.

A responsible law abiding citizen must know exactly which anatomical targets will stun, incapacitate, disfigure, maim, or kill the adversary. Therefore, let's take a closer look at these targets and the medical implications of each one.

Kubotan Targets

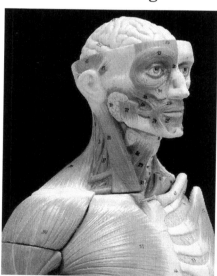

There are a specific collection of anatomical targets that you can either strike or apply pressure (as a pressure point) with a kubotan. Ideally, the best targets for kubotan strikes are bony surfaces that are only protected by a thin layer of skin as well as other soft tissue parts of the human body. What follows is a list of viable targets.

Eyes

The eyes are ideal targets for a kubotan attack because they are extremely sensitive and difficult to protect. The eyes can be poked, raked, and gouged from a variety of angles and vantages.

Depending on the force of your strike, it can cause numerous injuries, including watering of the eyes, hemorrhaging, blurred vision, temporary or permanent blindness, severe pain, rupture, shock, and even unconsciousness.

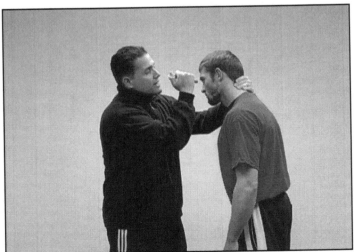

In this photo, the author delivers a kubotan strike to the eyes.

Temple

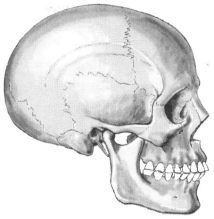

The temple or sphenoid bone is a thin, weak bone located on both sides of the skull approximately one inch from the assailant's eye. Because of its inherently weak structure and close proximity to the brain, a very powerful kubotan strike to this anatomical target can be deadly. Other possible injuries include unconsciousness, hemorrhaging, concussion, shock, and coma.

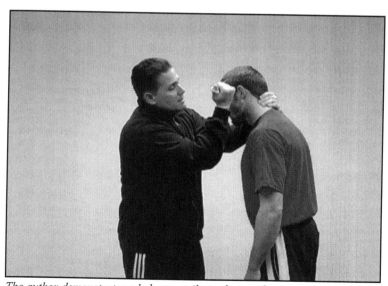

The author demonstrates a kubotan strike to the temple.

Nose

The nose is made up of a thin bone, cartilage, numerous blood vessels, and many nerves. It is a particularly good impact target because it stands out from the assailant's face and can be struck in three different directions (up, straight, down). A moderate blow can cause stunning pain, eye-watering, temporary blindness, and hemorrhaging. A powerful strike can result in shock and unconsciousness.

Chin

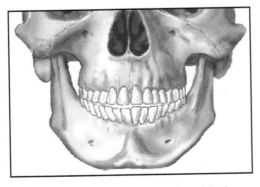

The chin is also a good target. When the chin is struck at a 45-degree angle, shock waves are transmitted to the cerebellum and cerebral hemispheres of the brain, resulting in paralysis and immediate unconsciousness.

Depending on the force of your blow, other possible injuries include broken jaw, concussion, and whiplash to the assailant's neck.

Back of Neck

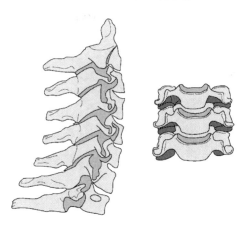

The back of the assailant's neck consists of the first seven vertebrae of the spinal column. They function as a circuit board for nerve impulses from the brain to the body. The back of the neck is a lethal target because the vertebrae are poorly protected. A very powerful strike to the back of the assailant's neck can cause shock, unconsciousness, a broken neck, complete paralysis, coma, and death.

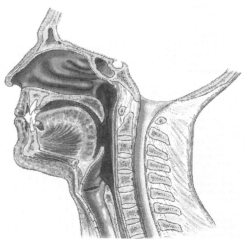

Back of the neck - side view.

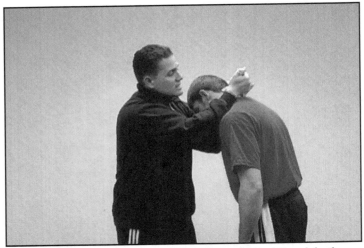

Striking the back of the neck should only be applied in life and death self-defense situations.

Spine

The spine or spinal column is also vulnerable to the kubotan. Like the back of the neck, the spine also functions as a circuit board for nerve impulses from the brain to the body.

A very powerful strike to the assailant's spine can cause shock, unconsciousness, complete paralysis, coma, and death.

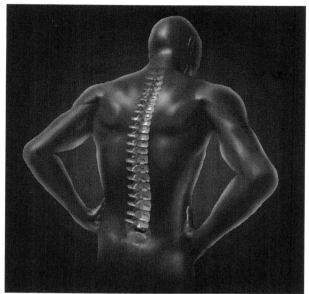

Like the back of the neck, the spine should only be struck in life and death self-defense situations.

Striking the spinal column.

Throat

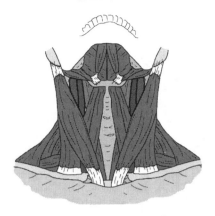

The throat is considered a lethal target because it is only protected by a thin layer of skin. This region consists of the thyroid, hyaline, cricoid cartilage, trachea, and larynx. The trachea, or windpipe, is a cartilaginous cylindrical tube that measure four and a half inches in length and approximately one inch in diameter.

A direct and powerful strike to this target may result in unconsciousness, blood drowning, massive hemorrhaging, strangulation, and death. If the thyroid cartilage is crushed, hemorrhaging will

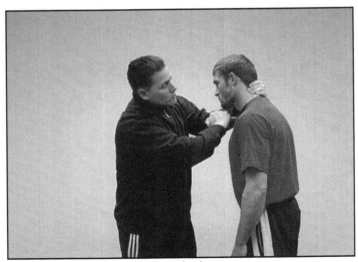

Striking the throat.

occur, the windpipe will quickly swell shut, and the assailant will die of suffocation.

Collarbone

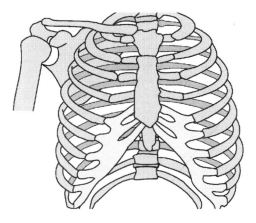

While the collar bone is not an ideal target for unarmed fighting, it's a great target for the kubotan. As a matter of fact, forcefully striking the collar bone with a kubotan can easily break it, resulting in extreme pain and difficulty moving the affected arm.

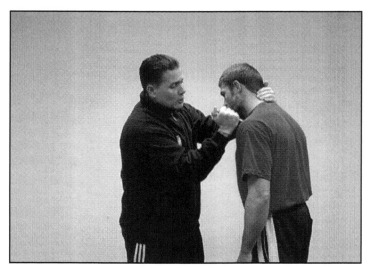

Striking the collarbone.

Ribs

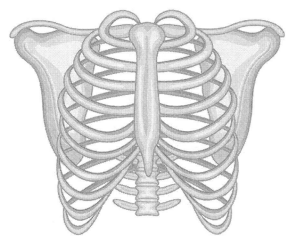

There are 12 pair of ribs in the human body. Excluding the 11th and 12th ribs, they are long and slender bones that are joined by the vertebral column in the back and the sternum and costal cartilage in the front. Since there are no 11th and 12th ribs (floating ribs) in the front, you should direct your strikes to the 9th and 10th ribs.

A moderate strike to the anterior region of the ribs may cause severe pain and shortness of breath. An extremely powerful 45-degree blow could break the assailant's rib and force it into a lung, resulting in the lung's collapse, internal hemorrhaging, air starvation, unconsciousness, excruciating pain, and possible death.

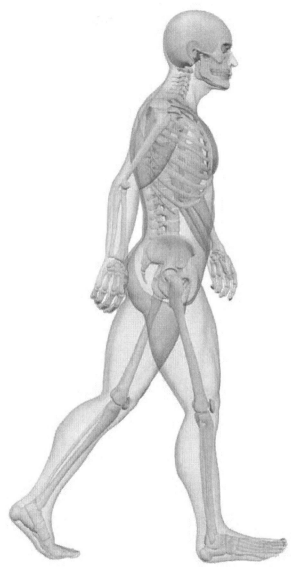

The human skeletal system offers ideal target opportunities for the kubotan. Attacking the skeletal system produces immediate results!

Solar Plexus

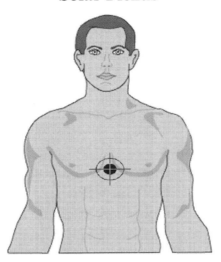

The solar plexus is a large collection of nerves situated below the sternum in the upper abdomen. A moderate blow to this area can cause nausea, pain, and shock, making it difficult for the adversary to breathe properly. A powerful strike to the solar plexus can result in severe abdominal pain and cramping, air starvation, and shock.

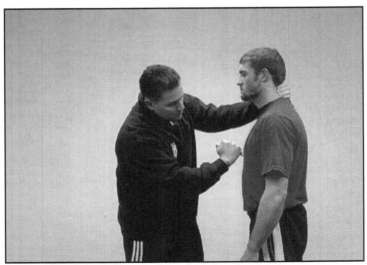

Pictured here, striking the solar plexus region.

Groin

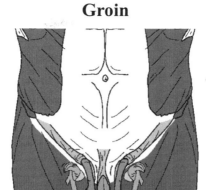

A moderate kubotan strike to an assailant's groin can cause a variety of possible reactions, including severe pain, nausea, vomiting, shortness of breath, and possible sterility. A powerful strike to the groin may crush the scrotum and the testes against the pubic bones, causing shock and unconsciousness.

Striking the groin.

Thighs

Since the thighs are large and muscular, they are *not* ideal striking targets for the kubotan. However, they are difficult to protect and make excellent striking targets for unarmed combat.

Although you can kick the thighs at a variety of different angles, the ideal location is the assailant's common peroneal nerve located on the side of the thigh, approximately four inches above the knee.

Striking this area can result in extreme pain and immediate immobility of the afflicted leg. An extremely hard kick to the thigh may result in a fracture of the femur, internal bleeding, severe pain, intense cramping, and long-term immobility.

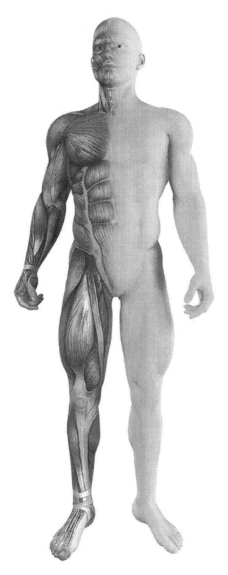

When striking your adversary with the kubotan, remember to hit bony targets that are only protected by a thin layer of skin. Avoid striking muscular parts of the body.

Knees

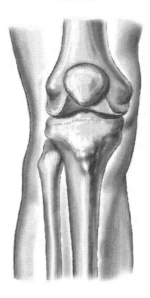

The knees are relatively weak joints that are held together by a number of supporting ligaments. When the assailant's leg is locked or fixed in position and a forceful strike is delivered to the front of the joint, the crucial ligaments will tear, resulting in excruciating pain, swelling, and immobility.

Located on the front of the knee joint is the kneecap, or patella, which is made of a small, loose piece of bone. The patella is also vulnerable to possible dislocation by a direct, forceful hit. Severe pain, swelling, and immobility may also result.

Shins

    The shins are also very sensitive targets because they are only protected by a thin layer of skin. A powerful blow delivered to this target may fracture it easily, resulting in extreme pain, hemorrhaging, and immobility of the afflicted leg.

Elbows

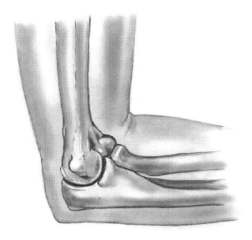

Because the elbows are only protected by a thin layer of skin, they are also ideal targets for the kubotan. Striking the elbow with a moderate amount of force can lead to immediate paralysis of the limb.

Striking the elbow.

Fingers and Hands

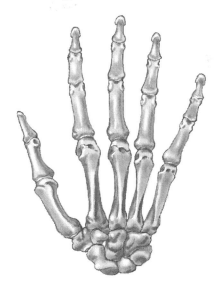

The fingers and hands are exceptionally weak and vulnerable and make ideal striking targets. The fingers can easily be jammed, sprained, broken, and torn. While a broken hand might not stop a determined fighter, it will certainly force him to release his hold.

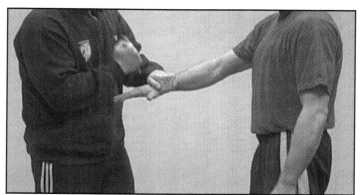

The back of the hands are extremely vulnerable to kubotan strikes.

Use-of-Force Considerations

One of the most difficult aspects of using a kubotan in a self-defense situation is determining exactly how much force can be applied. Well, since every self-defense situation is unique, there is no simple answer.

First, you must never use force against another person unless it is absolutely justified in the eyes of the law. Basically, use-of-force is broken down into two levels: lethal and nonlethal.

Lethal force is defined as the amount of force that can cause serious bodily injury or death. Nonlethal force is an amount of force that does not cause serious bodily injury or death.

Keep in mind that any time you use physical force against another person, you run the risk of having a civil suit filed against you. Remember, anyone can hire a lawyer and file a suit for damages. Likewise, anyone can file a criminal complaint against you. Whether criminal charges will be brought against you depends upon the prosecutor's or grand jury's view of the facts.

Second, a kubotan should only be used as an act of protection against unlawful injury or the immediate risk of unlawful injury. If you decide to strike your adversary with a kubotan, you'd better be certain that a reasonable threat exists and that it is absolutely necessary to protect yourself from immediate danger. Remember, the decision to use a self-defense weapon must always be a last resort, after all other means of avoiding violence have been exhausted.

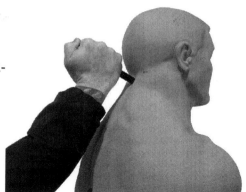

The back of the neck is considered a lethal target that should only be struck in of deadly force situations.

With that being said, there are two primary factors that determine the lethality of a kubotan strike. They are:

- **The anatomical target that you select.**
- **The amount of force you deliver to the intended target.**

The following chart will give you an idea of which anatomical targets are considered to be lethal.

Lethal Targets	Nonlethal Targets
Eyes	Nose
Temple	Chin
Throat	Collarbone
Back of Neck	Ribs
Spine	Solar Plexus
	Groin
	Knees
	Shins
	Elbows
	Hands

Developing Target Orientation with the Kubotan

The most effective way for developing target orientation is to practice kubotan strikes on the body opponent bag or BOB.

The body opponent bag is a self-standing lifelike punching bag designed to withstand tremendous punishment by allowing you to attack it with a wide variety of offensive techniques.

Because of its lifelike features, the body opponent bag is ideal for developing accuracy with the kubotan. The following photos will show you the various kubotan targets on the bag.

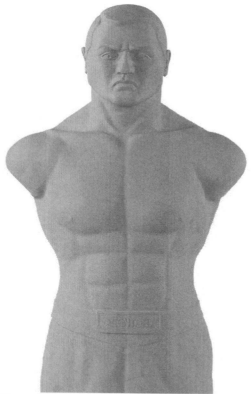

When it comes to target orientation with the kubotan, the body opponent bag is indispensable.

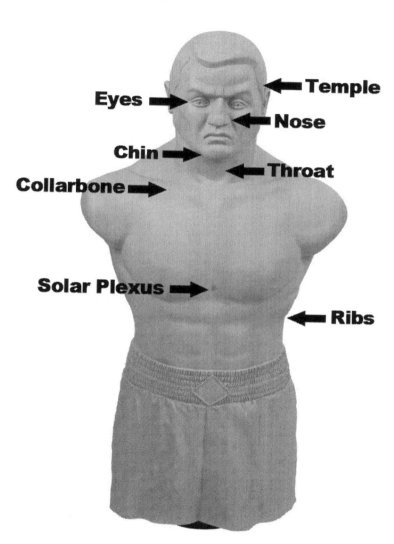

Front view targets.

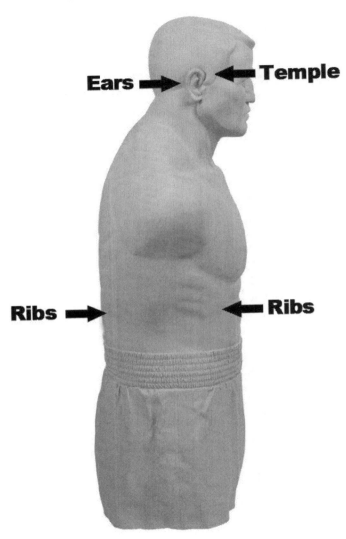

Side view targets.

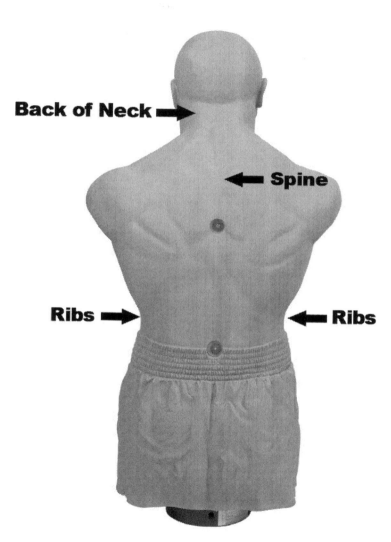

Rear view targets.

Body Opponent Bag Demonstrations

In this photo, the author uses a modified ice pick grip to deliver a kubotan strike to temple of the body opponent bag.

Pictured here, striking the collarbone on the body opponent bag.

Striking the eyes with the kubotan.

Striking the throat.

Target Recognition

The next component of target awareness is called target recognition. Target Recognition is the ability to immediately recognize specific kubotan targets during the actual confrontation, including both the pre-contact and contact stages of self-defense.

Target recognition is the ability to see anatomical targets during an actual self-defense encounter. How many kubotan targets do you see in this photo?

As I discussed earlier, the best targets are sensitive bony and soft tissue parts of the body like the eyes, temple, nose, chin, back of neck, throat, hands, etc.

Target recognition requires that you keep your calm during the duress of a combat situation and maintain a complete visual picture of your adversary.

One of the biggest mistakes that you can make during a fight is to gaze or stare into your opponent's eyes. Looking steadily into the assailant's eyes will significantly restricts your ability to recognize target opportunities during a fight.

One of the best ways to develop target recognition is to regularly participate in role-playing scenarios that replicate the stress of a real-world self-defense situations. A good reality based self-defense instructor can help you with this.

Target Selection

The third component of target awareness is target selection. When using a kubotan, never strike the opponent with reckless abandon. All of your blows must be smart and calculated. Target selection is the cognitive process of selecting the appropriate anatomical target to strike in combat.

Selecting the appropriate kubotan target is predicated on three important factors:

1. **Proximity of Opponent** - how far is the opponent from your kubotan?

2. **Positioning of Opponent** - exactly where is the opponent positioned and at what angle and height from the kubotan?

3. **Use of Force** - the amount of force (non-deadly or deadly) that is legally warranted for this particular self-defense situation. Remember, not every self-defense situation will warrant using deadly force. This means, that you are not permitted or justified to strike deadly force targets. Deadly force targets include the eyes, temple, throat, back of neck, and the spinal column.

Would you say this qualifies as a deadly force self-defense situation?

87

Target Impaction

Target Impaction is the physical process of striking the selected target with your weapon. Target impaction requires that each and every blow be delivered with maximum speed and power and minimal telegraphing. Proper attribute development will ensure successful target impaction during a confrontation.

Again, practicing regularly on the body opponent bag will help you develop the necessary speed and power required for effective striking technique.

Successful target impaction requires you to practice your kubotan techniques on a consistent basis. Remember, repetition is the mother of skill!

Target Exploitation

Finally, once you have acquired target impaction, you can implement target exploitation. Target exploitation is a combative attribute that allows you to strategically exploit your assailant's reaction dynamics during the altercation.

For example, let's say in the course of a self-defense situation, you successfully strike your opponent in the solar plexus with your kubotan. The impact from your strike causes the adversary to bend forward in pain. The opponent's physical action of bending over is called a "reaction dynamic." Target exploitation allows you to take advantage of the opponent's reaction dynamic by following up with another logical strike. In this case, a knee strike to the face would be a great follow up technique.

Other Kubotan Attributes

While target awareness is a vital attribute for kubotan deployment, there are others that are important and certainly worth mentioning.

Speed

In both armed and unarmed fighting you have to be fast- real fast! Your offensive and defensive techniques must move like a flash of lightening.

Actually, speed is a chief fighting attribute necessary for reality based self-defense. What most people don't realize is, fighting speed is something that you can easily improve. There are specific drills and exercises or "speed training" that can dramatically boost the quickness of your kubotan techniques as well as other fighting moves.

Combat speed is much like a steel chain made up of several separate links that are related to one another. Each link in the combat speed chain represents a particular component or unique attribute of quickness that must be practiced to maximize the overall acceleration of your martial arts skills and abilities.

One of the most effective methods of enhancing the physical speed of your kubotan techniques is to avoid tensing your body and simply relaxing your muscles prior to executing your movement.

Another way of developing blistering speed is to practice a particular kubotan strike thousands of times until the motor movement is sharpened and crystallized. I know this might sound boring, but I can assure you it produces great results.

Striking Power

When it come to real world self-defense, you must be capable of striking your opponent with knock-out force. To put it more bluntly, you've got to knock him on his ass!

Striking power refers to the amount of force you can generate when striking with a kubotan. Contrary to popular belief, striking power is not simply predicated on size, strength or body weight. There are other significant factors like power generator mastery, follow-through, and tool velocity that also play a critical role.

For example, one crucial factor of kubotan power is learning to develop proper technique or "body mechanics" and it can be accomplished through proper training.

Also, learning to use your three anatomical power generators will allow you to generate tremendous force when striking the adversary.

Essentially, power generators are specific points on your body which help generate impact power They are:

- **Feet**
- **Hips**
- **Shoulders**

Maximally torquing your body into the kubotan strike will significantly increase both the force and penetration of the blow.

Balance

Balance is the ability to maintain equilibrium while attacking and defending. You can maintain your balance in combat by controlling your center of gravity, mastering body mechanics and maintaining proper skeletal alignment.

To develop a better sense of balance, perform your kubotan strikes slowly in front of a mirror so you become acquainted with the different weight distributions, body positions, and mechanics of each particular technique.

Also, remember that balance is often lost due to weak body mechanics, poor kinesthetic perception, unnecessary weight shifting, excessive follow-through and improper skeletal alignment.

Non-Telegraphic Movement

It's critical not to telegraph or forewarn your opponent of your intentions to strike. Telegraphing means inadvertently making your offensive intentions known to your adversary.

In street self-defense, you must posses "clean" body mechanics that don't inform your adversary of your combative agenda. Basically, all of your movements have be non-telegraphic.

There are many forms of telegraphing which need to be purged from your kubotan arsenal. Here are a few examples:

- Staring at your selected target.
- Chambering your arm back before striking.
- Inadvertently showing your kubotan to your adversary.
- Tensing any part of your body.
- Grinning or opening your mouth.
- Widening your eyes or raising your eyebrows.
- Taking a sudden, deep breath.

Relaxation

Your body must be relaxed (but ready) during a threatening situation. You must also be free from muscular tension and the psychological pressure of combat. There are several effective ways to reduce nervous tension and enhance physical relaxation during a fight.

- **Preparation** - be prepared to handle the myriad of combat situations.

- **Proper breathing** - control and pace your breathing during the threatening encounter.

- **Fight-or-flight response** - learn to accept and control your fight-or-flight response during the altercation.

- **Proper attitude** - always maintain a positive attitude during a threatening situation.

- **Kinesthetic perception** - kinesthetic perception is important because it allows you to effectively regulate or monitor the muscular tension in your body.

Chapter Six
Defensive Techniques

The kubotan is a multi-purpose self-defense weapon that can be used for both offensive and defensive purposes. In this chapter, I will show you how to use it when defending against different types of street assaults. Let's begin with some basic wrist grabs.

One Hand Wrist Grab Defense
(Non Kubotan Hand)

In this scenario, the defender (left) assumes a low concealment position. The assailant (right) grabs his left wrist.

IMPORTANT: Since these photos are for demonstration purposes only, the defender will choke up on the tail of the kubotan so he won't injure his partner when he strikes the targets.

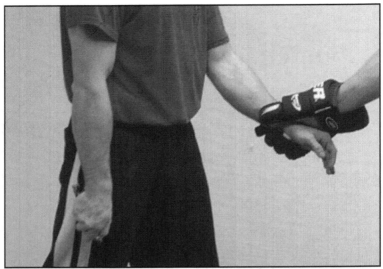

Step 1: The defender determines that a strike is justified.

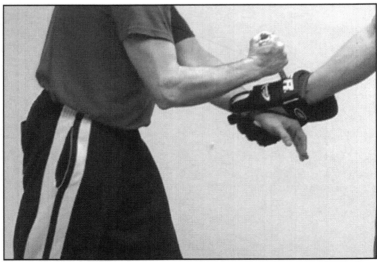

Step 2: The defender quickly counters the grab by striking repeatedly on the attacker's hand.

Step 3: Once the attacker releases his hold, the defender steps back into a defensive position.

One Hand Wrist Grab Defense
(Kubotan Hand)

Step1: The defender (left) accidentally displays his kubotan to his attacker.

Step 2: The attacker reaches for the kubotan and grabs the defender's wrist.

Step 3: In one fluid motion, the defender raises both of his hands up.

Step 4: He breaks free from the grab by forcefully retracting his arm backwards.

Step 5: He quickly counters with a strike to the collarbone.

Two-Hand Wrist Grab Defense
(From High Concealment Position)

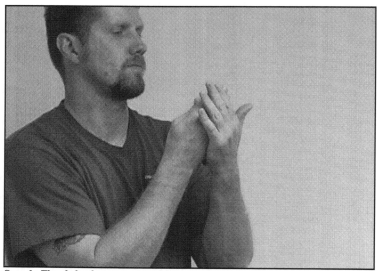

Step 1: The defender assumes a high concealment position.

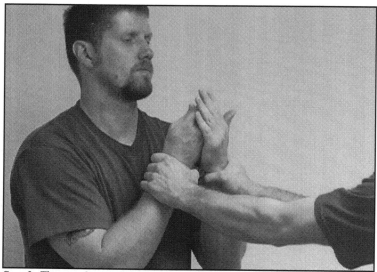

Step 2: The attacker grabs both of his wrists.

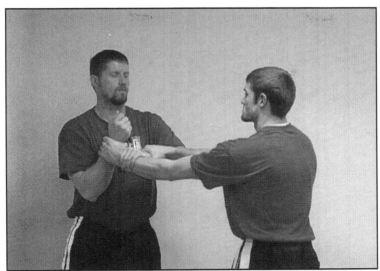

Step 3: The defender grabs the attackers wrist with his left hand.

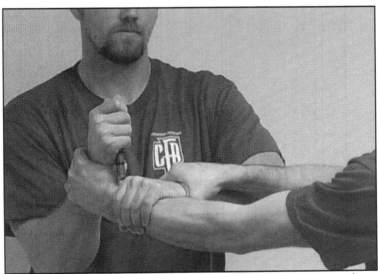

Step 4: Next, he lines up the tail of the kubotan with the attacker's wrist bone.

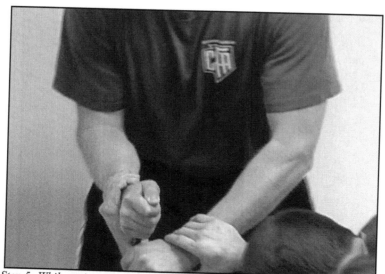

Step 5: While maintaining control of the attacker's wrist, he forcefully drives the kubotan downward.

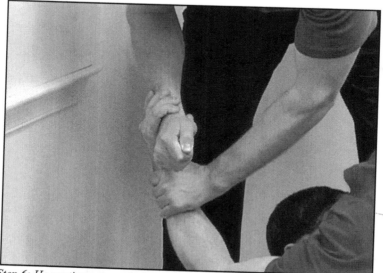

Step 6: He continues to push downward until the assailant is on his knees.

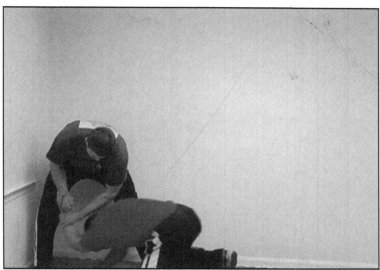

Step 7: At this point, the defender can either strike the assailant or escape from the situation.

Shirt Grab Defense
(Strike Counter)

Step 1: In this scenario, the defender (left) assumes a low concealment position.

Step 2: The assailant grabs the defender's shirt.

Step 3: The defender grabs and traps the assailant's wrist against his chest.

Step 4: Next, he forcefully strikes the attacker's elbow with the kubotan.

Notice how the defender maintains control of his assailant's wrist throughout the execution of the technique.

Step 5: The defender follows through with another strike to the elbow.

Step 6: The attacker quickly releases his grab and retracts his arm back.

Shirt Grab Defense
(Pain Compliance Counter)

Step 1: In this scenario, the defender (right) assumes a low concealment position.

Step 2: The assailant grabs his shirt.

Step 3: The defender places the kubotan over the attacker's wrist bone.

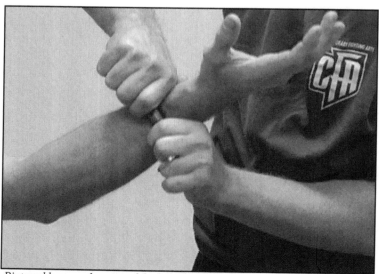

Pictured here, a close-up of the kubotan placement.

Step 4: Next, he forcefully squeezes the kubotan against the bone, forcing the assailant downward.

Step 5: The defender is now free to either strike the adversary or escape from the situation.

Two Hand Throat Choke Defense

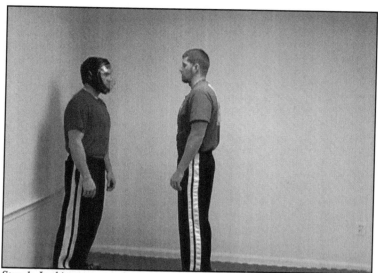

Step 1: In this scenario, the defender on the right assumes a low concealment position.

Step 2: The attacker reaches out and chokes the defender.

Step 3: In one fluid motion, the defender steps back with his left leg while trapping the assailant's right wrist. Next, swings his right arm over both of the attacker's arms. This position chambers and loads the kubotan for a strike.

Step 4: The defender strikes his attacker.

Step 5: The defender can follow up with another strike or escape from the situation.

Side Head Lock Defense

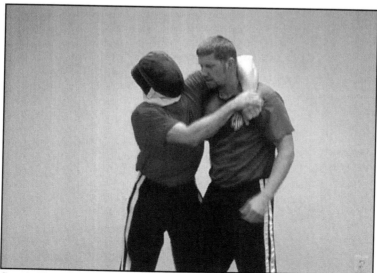

Step 1: The defender is placed in a side head lock.

Step 2: Before the attacker can solidify his hold, the defender turns his head inward and grabs hold of the assailant's wrists.

Step 3: Next, he swings his right arm up and over the attacker's head.

Step 4: He places the kubotan against the assailant's throat.

Step 5: He forces the assailant's head backward by driving the kubotan into his throat.

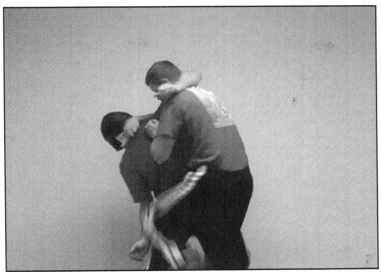

Step 6: He follows up with a knee strike.

Front Bear Hug Defense

Step 1: The defender (left) assumes a high concealment position.

Step 2: The attacker moves in with a front bear hug.

Step 3: The defender uses a reinforced ice pick grip and drives his kubotan into the assailant's sternum.

A close-up view of the reinforced ice pick grip.

Step 4: The assailant immediately releases his hold.

Step 5: The defender steps back and assumes a defensive position.

Rear Bear Hug Defense

Step 1: The defender is approached from behind.

Step 2: The attacker wraps his arms around the defender's body.

Step 3: The defender quickly bumps his hips backward while simultaneously widening his stance.

Step 4: The defender grabs hold of the assailant's left wrist.

Step 5: He strikes the attacker's hand with his kubotan.

Step 6: He continues to strike until the attacker loosens his hold.

Step 7: The defender grabs the assailant's finger and peels it backwards, allowing him to spin out of the hold.

Step 8: Once he is free, he follows up with another strike.

Escaping From The Leg Guard

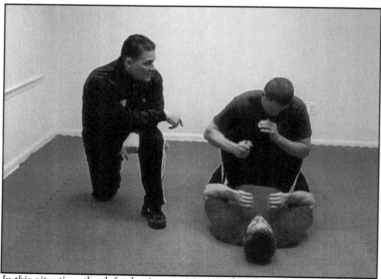

In this situation, the defender (top position) is placed in the opponent's leg guard.

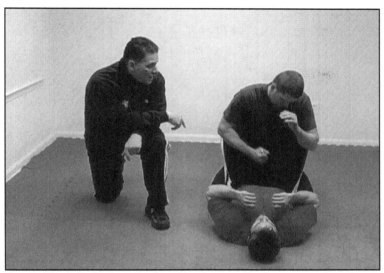

Step 1: The defender leans back and begins to strike the opponent's groin with the kubotan.

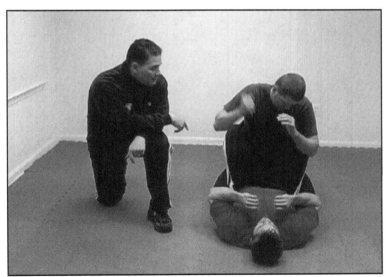

Step 2: He strikes again.

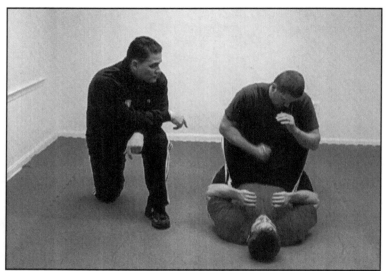

Step 3: And again.

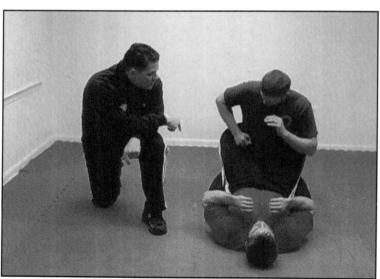

Step 4: The defender places the tail of the kubotan inside of the opponents leg.

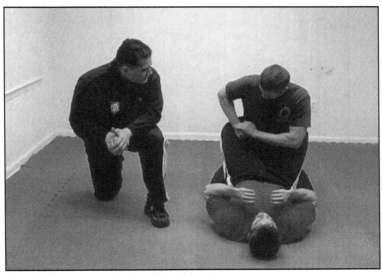

Step 5: He sets up a reinforced ice pick grip.

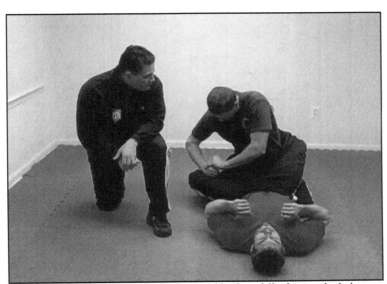

Step 6: The opponent's leg guard is opened by forcefully driving the kubotan downward.

Step 7: He holds the opponent's leg down.

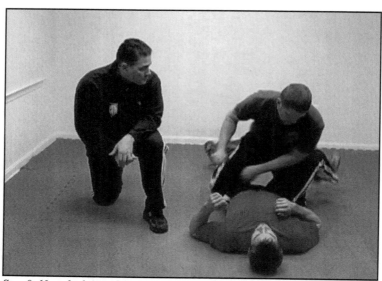

Step 8: Next, he brings his right knee over the opponent's leg.

Step 9: He does the same on the other side.

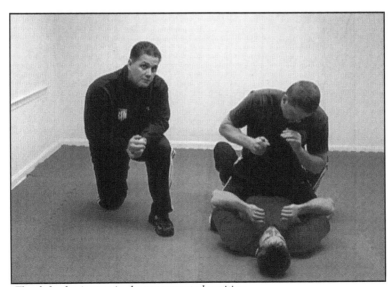

The defender is now in the top mounted position.

Kubotan Power

Chapter Seven
Training

Warming-Up & Stretching Out

Before training, it's important that you first warm up and stretch out. Warming up slowly increases the internal temperature of your body while stretching improves your workout performance, keeps you flexible, and helps reduce the possibility of an injury.

Some of the best exercises for warming up are jumping jacks, rope skipping or a short jog before training. Another effective method of warming up your muscles is to perform light and easy movements with the weights.

When stretching out, keep in mind that all movements should be performed in a slow and controlled manner. Try to hold your stretch for a minimum of sixty seconds and avoid all bouncing movements. You should feel mild tension on the muscle that is being stretched. Remember to stay relaxed and focus on what you are doing. Here are seven stretches that should be performed.

Neck stretch - from a comfortable standing position, slowly tilt your head to the right side of your neck, holding it for a count of twenty. Then tilt your head to the left side for approximately twenty seconds. Stretch each side of the neck at least three times.

Triceps stretch - from a standing position, keep your knees slightly bent, extend your right arm overhead, hold the elbow of your right arm with your left hand, and slowly pull your right elbow to the left. Keep your hips straight as you stretch your triceps gently for thirty seconds. Repeat this stretch for the other arm.

Hamstring stretch - from a seated position on the floor, extend your right leg in front of you with your toe pointing to the ceiling. Place the sole of your left foot in the inside of your extended leg. Gently lean forward at the hips and stretch out the hamstrings of your right leg. Hold this position for a minimum of sixty seconds. Switch legs and repeat the stretch.

Spinal twist - from a seated position on the floor, extend your right leg in front of you. Raise your left leg and place it to the outside of your right leg. Place your right elbow on the outside of your left thigh. Stabilize your stretch with your elbow and twist your upper body and head to your left side. Breathe naturally and hold this stretch for a minimum of thirty seconds. Switch legs and repeat this stretch for the other side.

Quad stretch - assume a sitting position on the floor with your hamstrings folded and resting on top of your calves. Your toes should be pointed behind you, and your instep should be flush with the ground. Sit comfortably into the stretch and hold for a minimum of sixty seconds.

Prone stretch - lay on the ground with your back to the floor. Exhale as you straighten your arms and legs. Your fingers and toes should be stretching in opposite directions. Hold this stretch for thirty seconds.

Groin stretch - sit on the ground with the soles of your feet touching each other. Grab hold of your feet and slowly pull yourself forward until mild tension is felt in your groin region. Hold this position for a minimum of sixty seconds.

Kubotan Combinations

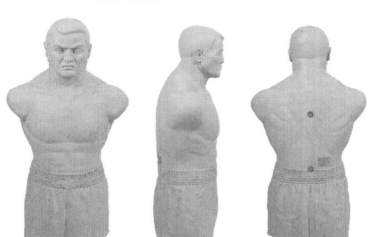

The best piece of equipment for developing kubotan striking combinations is the body opponent bag.

As I mentioned earlier, the body opponent bag is the best tool for developing striking proficiency with the kubotan. Because of it's life-like features, the body opponent bag will help you develop very accurate striking skills.

The following sequence of photos will show you the various target combinations you can perform on the bag. Remember to take your time when working out on the bag and work on developing the proper body mechanics before adding speed to your workout.

Also, one of the biggest mistakes you can make when working out on the body opponent bag, is to strictly hit the mannequin head on. Since kubotan targets are located on all sides of the bag, you should take full advantage and move around it when training.

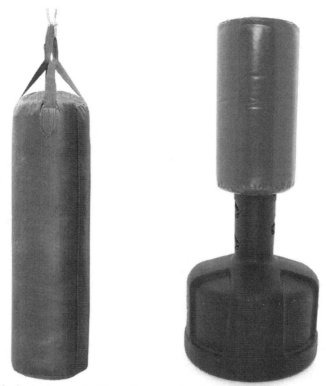

Both the heavy bag and self standing punching bag are poor choices for kubotan training. Remember, if you want to become accurate with your kubotan, then you will need to practice on a target specific bag.

Warning!

Before you begin any workout program, including those suggested in this book, it is important to check with your physician to see whether you have any condition that might be aggravated by strenuous exercise.

Kubotan Striking Combinations
(Front Targets)

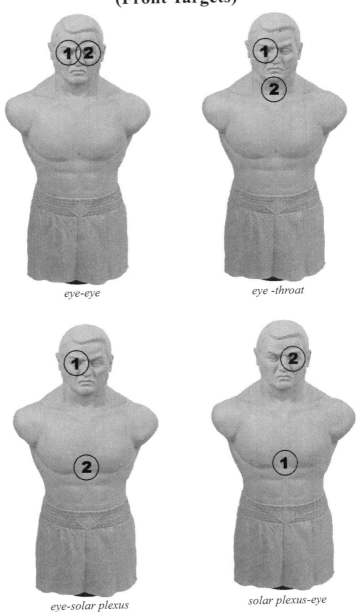

eye-eye   eye -throat

eye-solar plexus   solar plexus-eye

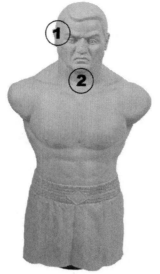

temple-throat

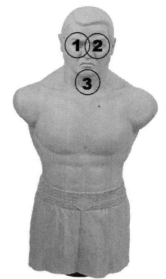

eye-eye-throat

eye-eye-solar plexus

temple-temple

temple-solar plexus

temple-temple-throat

temple-temple-solar plexus

temple-temple-collarbone -collarbone

Kubotan Power

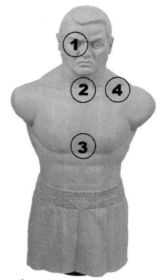

temple-solar plexus-collarbone-collarbone

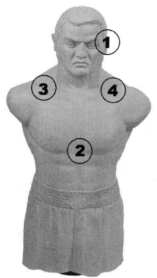

eye-throat-solar plexus-collarbone

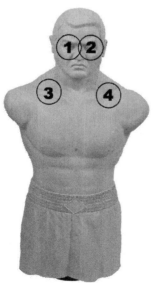

eye-eye-collarbone-collarbone

eye-chin-temple-throat

eye-collarbone-eye-collarbone

eye-solar plexus-groin

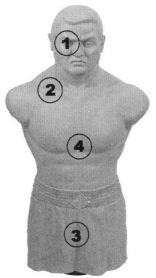

eye-collarbone-groin-solar plexus

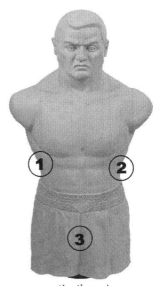

rib-rib-groin

Kubotan Power

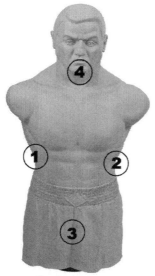

rib-rib-groin-chin

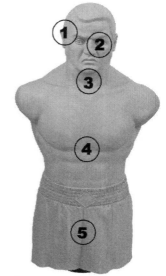

temple-eye-throat-solar plexus-groin

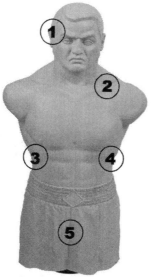

temple-collarbone-rib-rib-groin

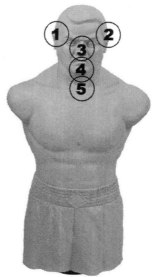

temple-temple-nose-chin-throat

Kubotan Striking Combinations
(Rear Targets)

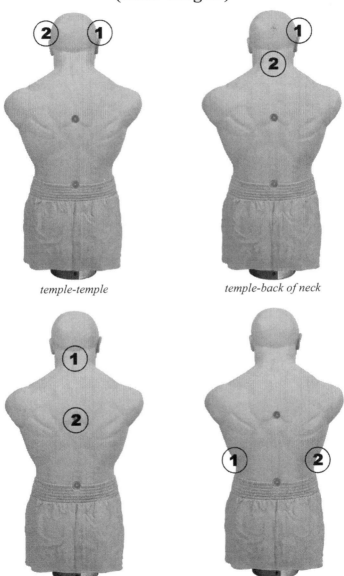

temple-temple

temple-back of neck

back of neck-spine

rib-rib

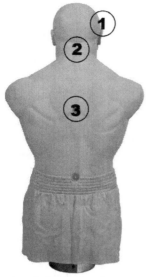

temple-back of neck-spine

back of neck-spine-lower spine

temple-back of neck-spine-lower spine

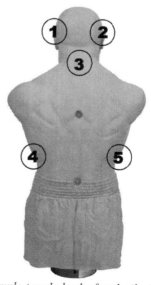

temple-temple-back of neck-rib-rib

Kubotan Striking Combinations
(Side Targets)

temple-throat

temple-throat-back of neck

temple-eye-throat

temple-eye-throat-back of neck

Kubotan Power

temple-eye-back of neck-solar plexus

rib-solar plexus-throat

rib-solar plexus-spine

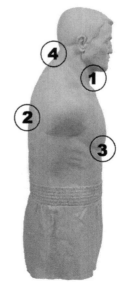

throat-spine-solar plexus-back of neck

Write Your Own Combinations

Use this section to write down your own kubotan combinations:

1.

2.

3.

4.

5.

6.

7.

8.

9.

10.

11.

12.

13.

14.

15.

16.

17.

18.

19.

20.

21.

22.

23.

24.

24.

26.

27.

28.

29.

30.

31.

32.

33.

34.

35.

36.

37.

38.

39.

40.

Kubotan Flow Drills

You can improve your kubotan skills by adding flow drills to your training. Flow drills are excellent for developing timing, speed and target accuracy. Here are a few exercises to get you started.

Hubod Drill

Step: 1 In this photo, the two practitioners begin the hubod drill with the man on the left initiating a tight overhead kubotan strike. The man on the right blocks the hit.

Step 2: After blocking the hit, the man on the right uses his right arm to redirect his partner's striking arm.

Step 3: As the man on the right redirects his partners arm and slaps it downward with his left hand.

Step 4: The man on the right then strikes his partner with a tight overhead kubotan strike.

144

Step 5: Next, the man on the left blocks his partner's hit and redirects it with his right arm.

Step 6: As he redirects his partners arm, he slaps it downward with his left hand.

Step 7: The cycle is complete and the man on the left begins again with a tight overhead kubotan strike.

Fist Loading Drill

Next, is the fist loading drill which helps improve your ability to deliver fisted blows with the kubotan in your hand.

Step1: Begin by squaring off with your partner with the back of your forearms touching each other.

Step 2: The man on the right begins the drill by slapping his partner's forearm while simultaneously punching with his right hand.

Step 3: The man (left) parries the punch with his left hand and redirects it with his right hand.

Step 4: As he redirects his partners arm, he slaps it downward with his left hand.

Step 5: He counters with a vertical punch directed to his partner's face.

Step 6: The man on the right parries the punch with his left hand and redirects it with his right hand.

Step 7: He slaps it downward with his left hand. The cycle is complete.

Back Hand Drill

Step 1: The two men square off with each other.

Step 2: Next, the man on the left delivers a controlled kubotan strike towards his partner's face. His partner intercepts the strike with the palm of his hand.

Step 3: The man on the right redirects his partner's arm downward.

Step 4: And counters with a strike to his partner's face.

Step 5: The man on the left intercepts his partner's strike and redirects it downward.

Step 6: The cycle is complete with the man on the left delivering a strike.

Combining Flow Drills

Now, it's time to combine all three flow drills together. Keep in mind, this is done arbitrarily with no set pattern. Remember, your goal is to flow with the kubotan, so keep it alive and dynamic!

Step 1: The man on the right begins by starting off with hubod.

Step 2: The man (right) initiates a tight overhead kubotan strike. The man on the left blocks the hit.

Step 3: Next, the man on the left redirects his partner's strike.

Step 4: He slaps his partner's arm downward.

Step 5: He counters with a tight overhead kubotan strike. The man on the right blocks the hit.

Step 6: The man on the right redirects his partner's arm.

Step 7: And slaps it.

Step 8: Next, the man on the right flows into the fist loading drill by delivering a vertical punch at his partner's face.

Step 9: The man on the left parries the punch and redirects it with his right hand.

Step 10: He counters with a vertical punch at his partner.

Step 11: The man on the right parries the punch with left hand.

Step 12: The man on the right transitions to the back hand drill.

Step 13: The man on the left intercepts his partner's strike and redirects it downward.

Step 14: He counters with a strike.

Step 15: The man on the right intercepts the strike.

Step 16: He counters with an overhead strike, transitioning back to the hubod drill.

Target Orientation Drill

The target orientation drill is designed to improve your awareness of target locations. The drill requires your partner to call out arbitrary kubotan targets and you must rapidly deploy the appropriate strike to the target. ***Warning! This is just an orientation drill, so be certain not to make contact with your partner's targets.***

Beginners should perform this drill with a modified ice pick grip and for a duration of two minutes. Once complete, switch the kubotan to your other hand and perform another two minute round. A good workout would be four to five sets.

When you become proficient with this exercise, you can perform the drill with the different types of kubotan grips. The following photo sequence shows the drill in action.

Begin the drill with the kubotan held in your dominant hand using either an ice pick or modified ice pick grip.

Your partner calls out, "Eye."

Your partner calls out, "Throat."

Your partner calls out, "Temple."

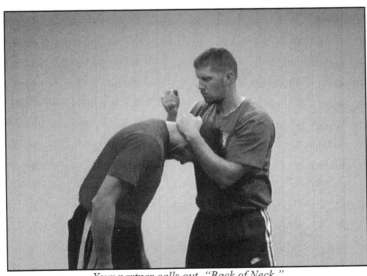

Your partner calls out, "Back of Neck."

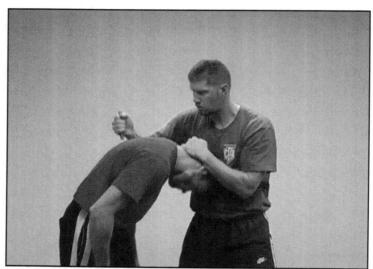

Your partner calls out, "Spine."

Your partner calls out, "Solar Plexus."

Your partner calls out, "Collarbone."

Your partner calls out, "Groin."

Your partner calls out, "Elbow."

Your partner calls out, "Hand."

More Kubotan Training Tips

- Before you begin your workout program, make certain that you have been cleared by your doctor. Since there is always some risk involved in training and because each person is unique, it is important that before beginning any type of training program, you should have a complete physical examination by your physician.

- Before working out with the kubotan, always warm up with some light stretching and calisthenics.

- Always start off with light strikes on the body opponent bag. Never go "all out" in the beginning of your workout session.

- When hitting the body opponent bag, never sacrifice proper technique for power or speed.

- Avoid wearing watches and jewelry when training.

- Consider shadow boxing with light dumbbells to strengthen your arm and shoulders for kubotan work.

- Never hold your breath. Remember to exhale with the delivery of every technique.

- If you don't know the proper way to deliver a kubotan strike, get instruction from a qualified instructor.

- Avoid locking out your elbows when striking the bag.

- Be mobile when working out on the bag, avoid the tendency to just stand and strike.

- The BOB doesn't hit back, so be aware of your own target openings and vulnerabilities when working out with the kubotan.

- Never let children play with a kubotan, especially one that has a pointed tip.

- Remember to maintain your balance always when performing striking techniques - never sacrifice your balance for power.

- When striking with the kubotan, learn to relax and avoid unnecessarily tensing your arm and shoulder muscles. Muscular tension will throw off the timing of your strikes.

- Try to be constantly aware of your form when striking with your kubotan. Perhaps, have a training partner observe you when working out on the bag. Another suggestion is to video tape yourself using the kubotan. This will give you a good idea of what you are doing in your workouts.

- Avoid burn out, don't engage in BOB training more than three times per week.

- Get into the habit of regularly inspecting your kubotan for signs of wear.

- Every so often, some cleaver marketing company will come up with a trendy gimmick claiming its just as good or better than a kubotan. Avoid it! The kubotan has been around for a very long time and is a tried a true self-defense weapon.

- Don't horse around with your kubotan. It's a self-defense weapon that should be treated with respect.

- When purchasing a kubotan, be certain its meets the specs and requirements discussed in this book.

- When looking to buy a kubotan, spare no expense. A high-quality kubotan will provide years of reliable use and enhance your self-defense skills.

More Kubotan Resources

If you would like to learn more about the kubotan, be sure to check out some of my other sources, available on our website and Amazon.com.

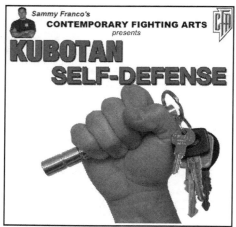

Kubotan Self-Defense DVD

Kubotan Video Download

Glossary of Terms

The following terms are defined in the context of Contemporary Fighting Arts and its related concepts. In many instances, the definitions bear little resemblance to those found in a standard dictionary.

A

Accuracy - The precise or exact projection of force. Accuracy is also defined as the ability to execute a combative movement with precision and exactness.

Adaptability - The ability to physically and psychologically adjust to new or different conditions or circumstances of combat.

Aerobic Exercise - "With air." Exercise that elevates the heart rate to a training level for a prolonged period of time, usually 30 minutes.

Agility - An attribute of combat. One's ability to move his or her body quickly and gracefully.

Ambidextrous - The ability to perform with equal facility on both the right and left sides of the body.

Attributes of Combat - The physical, mental, and spiritual qualities that enhance combat skills and tactics.

B

Balance - One's ability to maintain equilibrium while stationary or moving.

Blading the Body - Strategically positioning your body at a

45-degree angle.

BOB - (See body opponent bag.)

Body Mechanics - Technically precise body movement during the execution of a body weapon, defensive technique, or other fighting maneuver.

Body Opponent Bag - (also known as BOB). A self standing, body-shaped punching bag constructed of synthetic rubber material called plastisol. The body opponent bag is comprised of two separate parts: the torso and base.

Body Weapon - (also known as tool). One of the various body parts that can be used to strike or otherwise injure or kill a criminal assailant.

Burn Out – A negative emotional state acquired by physically over training. Some symptoms include: illness, boredom, anxiety, disinterest in training, and general sluggishness.

C

Cadence - Coordinating tempo and rhythm to establish a timing pattern of movement.

Cardiorespiratory Conditioning - The component of physical fitness that deals with the heart, lungs, and circulatory system.

Centerline - An imaginary vertical line that divides your body in half and which contains many of your vital anatomical targets.

Circular Movement - Movements that follow the direction of a curve.

Clinching - Strategically locking up with the adversary while you are standing.

Close Quarter Combat - One of the three ranges of knife and bludgeon combat. At this distance, you can strike, slash, or stab your assailant with a variety of close-quarter techniques.

Cognitive Development - One of the five elements of CFA's mental component. The process of developing and enhancing your fighting skills through specific mental exercises and techniques. (See analysis and integration, killer instinct, philosophy and strategic/tactical development.)

Combat Oriented Training – Training that is specifically related to the harsh realities of both armed and unarmed combat. (see ritual oriented training and sport oriented training.)

Combative Arts - The various arts of war. (See martial arts.)

Combative Attributes - (See attributes of combat.)

Combative Fitness - A state characterized by cardiorespiratory and muscular/skeletal conditioning, as well as proper body composition.

Combat Ranges - The various ranges of unarmed combat.

Combative Utility - The quality of condition of being combatively useful.

Combination(s) - (See compound attack.)

Compound Attack - One of the five conventional methods of attack. Two or more body weapons launched in strategic succession whereby the fighter overwhelms his assailant with a flurry of full speed, full force blows.

Conditioning Training - A CFA training methodology requiring the practitioner to deliver a variety of offensive and defensive combinations for a four minute period (See proficiency training and street training.)

Contemporary Fighting Arts® (CFA) - A modern martial art and self-defense system made up of three parts: physical, mental, and spiritual.

Coordination - A physical attribute characterized by the ability to perform a technique or movement with efficiency, balance, and accuracy.

Counterattack - Offensive action made to counter an assailant's initial attack.

Cross Stepping - The process of crossing one foot in front or behind the other when moving.

D

Defense - The ability to strategically thwart an assailant's attack (armed or unarmed).

Diet - A life-style of healthy eating.

Distancing - The ability to quickly understand spatial relationships and how they relate to combat.

Double-End Bag – A small leather ball suspended in the air by bungee cord which develops striking accuracy, speed, timing, eye-hand coordination, footwork and overall defensive skills.

E

Effectiveness - One of the three criteria for a CFA body weapon, technique, tactic or maneuver. It means the ability to produce a desired effect (See efficiency and safety.)

Efficiency - One of the three criteria for a CFA body weapon, technique, tactic or maneuver. It means the ability to reach an objective quickly and economically (see effectiveness and safety.)

Evasion - A defensive maneuver that allows you to strategically maneuver your body away from the assailant's strike.

Evasive Sidestepping - Evasive footwork where the practitioner moves to either the right or left side.

Evasiveness - A combative attribute. The ability of avoid threat or danger.

Excessive Force - An amount of force that exceeds the need for a particular event and is unjustified in the eyes of the law.

Experimentation - The painstaking process of testing a combative hypothesis or theory.

Explosiveness - A combative attribute that is characterized by a sudden outburst of violent energy.

F

Fighting Stance - One of the different types of stances used in CFA's system. A strategic posture you can assume when face-to-face with an unarmed assailant (s). The fighting stance is generally used after you have launched your first strike tool.

Finesse - A combative attribute. The ability to skillfully execute a movement or a series of movements with grace and refinement.

Fisted blows – Hand blows delivered with a clenched fist.

Fist loading - The process of delivering fisted blows with kubotan in your hand.

Flexibility - The muscles' ability to move through maximum natural ranges (See muscular/skeletal conditioning.)

Focus Mitts – Durable leather hands mitts used to develop and sharpen offensive and defensive skills.

Footwork - Quick, economical steps performed on the balls of the feet while you are relaxed, alert, and balanced. Footwork is structured around four general movements: forward, backward, right, and left.

G

Grappling Range - One of the three ranges of unarmed combat. Grappling range is the closest distance of unarmed combat from which you can employ a wide variety of close-quarter tools and techniques. The grappling range of unarmed combat is also divided into two different planes: vertical (standing) and horizontal (ground fighting). (See kicking range and punching range.)

Grappling Range Tools - The various body tools and techniques that are employed in the grappling range of unarmed combat, including head butts; biting, tearing, clawing, crushing, and gouging tactics; foot stomps, horizontal, vertical, and diagonal elbow strikes, vertical and diagonal knee strikes, chokes, strangles, joint locks, and holds. (See punching range tools and kicking range tools.)

H

Hand Positioning - (See guard.)

Hand Wraps – Long strips of cotton that are wrapped around the hands and wrists for greater protection.

Head-Hunter - A fighter who primarily attacks the head.

Heavy Bag - A large cylindrical shaped bag that is used to develop kicking, punching or striking power.

High-Line Kick - One of the two different classifications of a kick. A kick that is directed to targets above an assailant's waist level. (See low-line kick.)

Hook Kick - A circular kick that can be delivered in both kicking and punching ranges.

Hook Punch - A circular punch that can be delivered in both the punching and grappling ranges.

I

Impact Power - Destructive force generated by mass and velocity.

Incapacitate - To disable an assailant by rendering him unconscious or damaging his bones, joints or organs.

J

Jiu-jitsu – Translates to "soft/pliable". Jiu-jitsu is a martial art developed in feudal Japan that emphasizes throws, joint locks and weapons training.

Joint Lock - A grappling range technique that immobilizes the assailant's joint.

Judo - Translates to "gentle/soft way". Judo is an Olympic sport which originated in Japan.

K

Kick - A sudden, forceful strike with the foot.

Kicking Range - One of the three ranges of unarmed combat. Kicking range is the furthest distance of unarmed combat wherein you use your legs to strike an assailant. (See grappling range and punching range.)

Kicking Range Tools - The various body weapons employed in the kicking range of unarmed combat, including side kicks, push kicks, hook kicks, and vertical kicks.

Kubotan - A close-quarter self-defense weapon.

L

Lead Side - The side of the body that faces an assailant.

Linear Movement - Movements that follow the path of a straight line.

Low Maintenance Tool - Offensive and defensive tools that require the least amount of training and practice to maintain proficiency. Low maintenance tools generally do not require preliminary stretching.

Low-Line Kick - One of the two different classifications of a kick. A kick that is directed to targets below the assailant's waist level. (See high-line kick.)

Lock - (See joint lock.)

M

Maneuver - To manipulate into a strategically desired position.

Martial arts - The "arts of war".

Mechanics - (See body mechanics.)

Mental Attributes - The various cognitive qualities that enhance your fighting skills.

Mental Component - One of the three vital components of the CFA system. The mental component includes the cerebral aspects of fighting including the Killer Instinct, Strategic & Tactical Development, Analysis & Integration, Philosophy and Cognitive Development (See physical component and spiritual component.)

Mixed Martial Arts - Also known as MMA, is a concept of fighting where the practitioner integrates a variety of fighting styles into a single method of fighting that can be tested in a regulated full-contact combat sport.

Mobility - A combative attribute. The ability to move your body quickly and freely while balanced. (See footwork.)

Modern Martial Art - A pragmatic combat art that has evolved to meet the demands and characteristics of the present time.

Muscular Endurance - The muscles' ability to perform the same motion or task repeatedly for a prolonged period of time.

Muscular Flexibility - The muscles' ability to move through maximum natural ranges.

Muscular Strength - The maximum force that can be exerted by a particular muscle or muscle group against resistance.

Muscular/Skeletal Conditioning - An element of physical fitness that entails muscular strength, endurance, and flexibility.

N

Neutral Zone - The distance outside of the kicking range from which neither the practitioner nor the assailant can touch the other.

No Holds Barred Competition (NHB) – A sport competition with few rules.

Non telegraphic Movement - Body mechanics or movements that do not inform an assailant of your intentions.

O

Offense - The armed and unarmed means and methods of attacking a criminal assailant.

Offensive Flow - Continuous offensive movements (kicks, blows, and strikes) with unbroken continuity that ultimately neutralize or terminate the opponent. (See compound attack.)

Offensive Reaction Time (ORT) - The elapsed time between target selection and target impaction.

P

Pain Tolerance - Your ability to physically and psychologically withstand pain.

Parry - A defensive technique; a quick, forceful slap that redirects an assailant's linear attack. There are two types of parries: horizontal and vertical.

Patience - A combative attribute. The ability to endure and tolerate difficulty.

Perception - Interpretation of vital information acquired from your senses when faced with a potentially threatening situation.

Physical Attributes - The numerous physical qualities that enhance your combative skills and abilities.

Physical Component - One of the three vital components of the CFA system. The physical component includes the physical aspects of fighting including Physical Fitness, Weapon/Technique Mastery, and Combative Attributes. (See mental component and spiritual component.)

Physical Conditioning - (See combative fitness.)

Physical Fitness - (See combative fitness.)

Positioning - The spatial relationship of the assailant to the assailed person in terms of target exposure, escape, angle of attack, and various other strategic considerations.

Power - A physical attribute of armed and unarmed combat. The amount of force you can generate when striking an anatomical target.

Power Generators – Specific points on your body which generate impact power. There are three anatomical power generators: shoulders, hips, and feet.

Precision - (See accuracy.)

Preparedness – A state of being ready for combat. There are three components of preparedness: affective preparedness, cognitive preparedness and psychomotor preparedness.

Proficiency Training - A CFA training methodology requiring the practitioner to execute a specific body weapon, technique, maneuver or tactic over and over for a prescribed number or repetitions. (See conditioning training and street training.)

Proxemics - The study of the nature and effect of man's personal space.

Proximity - The ability to maintain a strategically safe distance from a threatening individual.

Psychological Conditioning - The process of conditioning the mind for the horrors and rigors of real combat.

Punch - A quick, forceful strike of the fists.

Punching Range - One of the three ranges of unarmed combat. Punching range is the mid range of unarmed combat from which the fighter uses his hands to strike his assailant. (See kicking range and grappling range.)

Punching Range Tools - The various body weapons that are employed in the punching range of unarmed combat, including finger jabs, palm heel strikes, rear cross, knife hand strikes, horizontal and shovel hooks, uppercuts, and hammer fist strikes. (See grappling range tools and kicking range tools.)

Q

Qualities of Combat - (See attributes of combat.)

R

Range - The spatial relationship between a fighter and a threatening assailant.

Range Deficiency - The inability to effectively fight and defend in all ranges (armed and unarmed) of combat.

Range Manipulation - A combative attribute. The strategic manipulation of combat ranges.

Range Proficiency - A combative attribute. The ability to effectively fight and defend in all ranges (armed and unarmed) of combat.

Ranges of Engagement - (See combat ranges.)

Ranges of Unarmed Combat - The three distances a fighter might physically engage with an assailant while involved in unarmed combat: kicking range, punching range, and grappling range.

Raze – To level, demolish or obliterate.

Razer – One who performs the Razing methodology.

Razing – The second phase of the WidowMaker Program. A series of vicious close quarter techniques designed to physically and psychologically extirpate a criminal attacker.

Reaction Dynamics - The assailant's physical response or reaction to a particular tool, technique, or weapon after initial contact is made.

Reaction Time - The elapsed time between a stimulus and the response to that particular stimulus (See offensive reaction time and defensive reaction time.)

Rear Cross - A straight punch delivered from the rear hand that crosses from right to left (if in a left stance) or left to right (if in a right stance).

Rear Side - The side of the body furthest from the assailant (See lead side.)

Refinement - The strategic and methodical process of improving or perfecting.

Repetition - Performing a single movement, exercise, strike or action continuously for a specific period.

Rhythm - Movements characterized by the natural ebb and flow of related elements.

S

Safety - One of the three criteria for a CFA body weapon, technique, maneuver or tactic. It means the that the tool, technique, maneuver or tactic provides the least amount of danger and risk for the practitioner (See efficiency and effectiveness.)

Self-Confidence - Having trust and faith in yourself.

Set - A term used to describe a grouping of repetitions.

Shadow Fighting - A CFA training exercise used to develop and refine your tools, techniques, and attributes of armed and unarmed combat.

Skeletal Alignment - The proper alignment or arrangement of your body. Skeletal Alignment maximizes the structural integrity of striking tools.

Skills – One of the three factors that determine who will win a street fight. Skills refers to psychomotor proficiency with the tools and techniques of combat. (See Attitude and Knowledge.)

Slipping - A defensive maneuver that permits you to avoid an assailant's linear blow without stepping out of range. Slipping can be accomplished by quickly snapping the head and upper torso sideways (right or left) to avoid the blow.

Snap Back - A defensive maneuver that permits you to avoid an assailant's linear and circular blow without stepping out of range. The snap back can be accomplished by quickly snapping the head backwards to avoid the assailant's blow.

Sparring – A training exercise where two (or more) fighters fight each other while wearing protective equipment.

Speed - A physical attribute of armed and unarmed combat. The rate or a measure of the rapid rate of motion.

Spiritual Component - One of the three vital components of the CFA system. The spiritual component includes the metaphysical issues and aspects of existence (See physical component and mental component.)

Sport Oriented Training – Training that is geared for competition that is governed by a set of rules. (See combat oriented training and ritual oriented training.)

Sprawling – A grappling technique used to counter a double or single leg takedown.

Square-Off - To be face-to-face with the body opponent bag.

Stance - One of the many strategic postures that you assume prior to or during armed or unarmed combat.

Strategic/Tactical development - One of the five elements of CFA's mental component.

Strategy - A carefully planned method of achieving your goal of engaging an assailant under advantageous conditions.

Street Fight - A spontaneous and violent confrontation between two or more individuals wherein no rules apply.

Street Fighter - An unorthodox combatant who has no formal training. His combative skills and tactics are usually developed in the street by the process of trial and error.

Street Training - A CFA training methodology requiring the practitioner to deliver explosive compound attacks for ten to twenty-seconds (See conditioning training and proficiency training.)

Strength Training - The process of developing muscular strength through systematic application of progressive resistance.

Striking Art - A combat art that relies predominantly on striking techniques to neutralize or terminate a criminal attacker.

Striking Tool - A natural body weapon that impacts with the assailant's anatomical target.

Strong Side - The strongest and most coordinated side of your body.

Structure - A definite and organized pattern.

Style - The distinct manner in which a fighter executes or performs his combat skills.

Stylistic Integration - The purposeful and scientific collection of tools and techniques from various disciplines, which are strategically integrated and dramatically altered to meet three essential criteria: efficiency, effectiveness, and combative safety.

Submission Hold – (also known as control and restraint techniques). Many of the locks and holds that create sufficient pain to cause the adversary to submit.

Submission Technique - Includes all locks, bars, and holds that cause sufficient pain to cause the adversary to submit.

System - The unification of principles, philosophies, rules, strategies, methodologies, tools, and techniques or a particular method of combat.

T

Tactic - The skill of using the available means to achieve an end.

Target Awareness - A combative attribute which encompasses 5 strategic principles: target orientation, target recognition, target selection, target impaction, and target exploitation.

Target Exploitation - A combative attribute. The strategic maximization of your assailant's reaction dynamics during a fight. Target Exploitation can be applied in both armed and unarmed encounters.

Target Impaction - The successful striking of the appropriate anatomical target.

Target Orientation - A combative attribute. Having a workable knowledge of the assailant's anatomical targets.

Target Recognition - The ability to immediately recognize appropriate anatomical targets during an emergency self-defense situation.

Target Selection - The process of mentally selecting the appropriate anatomical target for your self-defense situation. This is predicated on certain factors, including proper force response, assailant's positioning and range.

Technique - A systematic procedure by which a task is accomplished.

Telegraphing - Unintentionally making your intentions known to your adversary.

Tempo - The speed or rate at which you speak.

Timing - A physical and mental attribute or armed and unarmed combat. Your ability to execute a movement at the optimum moment.

Tool - (See body weapon.)

Traditional Martial Arts - Any martial art that fails to evolve and change to meet the demands and characteristics of its present environment.

Traditional Style/System - (See traditional martial art.)

Training Drills - The various exercises and drills aimed at perfecting combat skills, attributes, and tactics.

U

Unified Mind - A mind free and clear of distractions and focused on the combative situation.

Use of Force Response - A combative attribute. Selecting the appropriate level of force for a particular emergency self-defense situation.

V

Visualization – Also known as Mental Visualization or Mental Imagery. The purposeful formation of mental images and scenarios in the mind's eye.

W

Warm-up - A series of mild exercises, stretches, and movement designed to prepare you for more intense exercise.

Weak Side - The weakest and most uncoordinated side of your body.

Weapon and Technique Mastery - A component of CFA's physical component. The kinesthetic and psychomotor development of a weapon or combative technique.

Webbing - A reinforced palm heel strike primarily delivered to the assailant's chin. It is termed Webbing because your hands resemble a large web that wraps around the enemy's face.

WidowMaker Program – A fighting style created by Sammy Franco that is specifically designed to teach the law-abiding citizen how to use extreme force when faced with immediate threat of unlawful deadly criminal attack. The WidowMaker program is divided into two sections or phases: Webbing and Razing.

Y

Yell - A loud and aggressive scream or shout used for various strategic reasons.

Z

Zero Beat – One of the four beat classifications of the Widow-Maker Program. Zero beat strikes are full pressure techniques applied to a specific target until it completely ruptures. Zero beat tools include gouging, biting and choking techniques

Zone One - Anatomical targets related to your senses, including the eyes, temple, nose, chin, and back of neck.

Zone Two - Anatomical targets related to your breathing, including front of neck, solar plexus, ribs, and groin.

Zone Three - Anatomical targets related to your mobility, including thighs, knees, shins, and instep.

About The Author

Sammy Franco is one of the world's foremost authorities on armed and unarmed combat. Highly regarded as a leading innovator in combat sciences, Mr. Franco was one of the premier pioneers in the field of "reality-based" self-defense and martial arts instruction.

Convinced of the limited usefulness of martial arts in real street fighting situations, Mr. Franco believes in the theory that the best way to change traditional thinking is to make antiquated ideas obsolete through superior methodology. His innovative ideas have made a significant contribution to changing the thinking of many in the field about how people can best defend themselves against vicious and formidable adversaries.

Sammy Franco is perhaps best known as the founder and creator of Contemporary Fighting Arts (CFA), a state-of-the-art offensive-based combat system that is specifically designed for real-world self-defense. CFA is a sophisticated and practical system of self-defense, designed specifically to provide efficient and effective methods to avoid, defuse, confront, and neutralize both armed and unarmed attackers.

After studying and training in numerous martial art systems and related disciplines and acquiring extensive firsthand experience from real "street" combat, Mr. Franco developed his first system, known as Analytical Street Fighting. This system, which was one of the first practical "street fighting" martial arts, employed an unrestrained reality-based training methodology known as Simulated Street Fighting. Analytical Street Fighting served as the foundation for the fundamental principles of Contemporary Fighting Arts and Mr. Franco's teaching methodology.

193

CFA also draws from the concepts and principles of numerous sciences and disciplines, including police and military science, criminal justice, criminology, sociology, human psychology, philosophy, histrionics, kinesics, proxemics, kinesiology, emergency medicine, crisis management, and human anatomy.

Sammy Franco has frequently been featured in martial art magazines, newspapers, and appeared on numerous radio and television programs. Mr. Franco has also authored numerous books, magazine articles and editorials, and has developed a popular library of instructional DVDs and workout music. As a matter of fact, his book Street Lethal was one of the first books ever published on the subject of reality based self-defense. His other books include Killer Instinct, When Seconds Count, 1001 Street Fighting Secrets, First Strike, The Bigger They Are – The Harder They Fall, War Machine, War Craft, Ground War, Warrior Wisdom, Out of the Cage, Gun Safety Handbook Heavy Bag Training and The Body Complete Body Opponent Bag Book.

Sammy Franco's experience and credibility in the combat science is unequaled. One of his many accomplishments in this field includes the fact that he has earned the ranking of a Law Enforcement Master Instructor, and has designed, implemented, and taught officer survival training to the United States Border Patrol (USBP). He instructs members of the US Secret Service, Military Special Forces, Washington DC Police Department, Montgomery County, Maryland Deputy Sheriffs, and the US Library of Congress Police. Sammy Franco is also a member of the prestigious International Law Enforcement Educators and Trainers Association (ILEETA) as well as the American Society of Law Enforcement Trainers (ASLET) and he is listed in the "Who's Who Director of Law Enforcement Instructors."

Sammy Franco is a nationally certified Law Enforcement Instructor in the following curricula: PR-24 Side-Handle Baton, Police Arrest and Control Procedures, Police Personal Weapons Tactics, Police Power Handcuffing Methods, Police Oleoresin Capsicum Aerosol Training (OCAT), Police Weapon Retention and Disarming Methods, Police Edged Weapon Countermeasures and "Use of Force" Assessment and Response Methods.

Mr. Franco is also a National Rifle Association (NRA) instructor who specializes in firearm safety, personal protection and advanced combat pistol shooting.

Mr. Franco holds a Bachelor of Arts degree in Criminal Justice from the University of Maryland. He is a regularly featured speaker at a number of professional conferences, and conducts dynamic and enlightening seminars on numerous aspects of self-defense and personal protection.

Mr. Franco has instructed thousands of students in his career, including instruction on street fighting, grappling and ground fighting, boxing and kick boxing, knife combat, multiple opponent survival skills, stick fighting, and firearms training. Having lived through street violence himself, Mr. Franco's goal is not its glorification, but to help people free themselves from violence and its costly price.

For more information about Mr. Franco and his unique Contemporary Fighting Arts system, you can visit his website at: www. sammyfranco.com

If you liked this book, you will also want to read these:

THE COMPLETE BODY OPPONENT BAG BOOK
by Sammy Franco

In this one-of-a-kind book, world-renowned martial arts expert, Sammy Franco teaches you the many hidden training features of the body opponent bag that will improve your fighting skills and accelerate your fitness and conditioning. Develop explosive speed and power, improve your endurance, and tone, and strengthen your entire body. With detailed photographs, step-by-step instructions, and dozens of unique workout routines, The Complete Body Opponent Bag Book is the authoritative resource for mastering this lifelike punching bag. 8.5 x 5.5, soft cover, photos, illustrations, 206 pages.

WAR MACHINE
How to Transform Yourself Into A Vicious & Deadly Street Fighter
by Sammy Franco

War Machine is a book that will change you for the rest of your life! When followed accordingly, War Machine will forge your mind, body and spirit into iron. Once armed with the mental and physical attributes of the War Machine, you will become a strong and confident warrior that can handle just about anything that life may throw your way. In essence, War Machine is a way of life. Powerful, intense, and hard. 11 x 8.5, soft cover, photos, illustrations, 210 pages.

OUT OF THE CAGE
A Complete Guide to Beating a Mixed Martial Artist on the Street
by Sammy Franco

Forget the UFC! The truth is, a street fight is the "ultimate no holds barred fight" often with deadly consequences, but you don't need to join a mixed martial arts school or become a cage fighter to defeat a mixed martial artist on the street. What you need are solid skills and combat proven techniques that can be applied under the stress of real world combat conditions. Out of the Cage takes you inside the mind of the MMA fighter and reveals all of his weaknesses, allowing you to quickly exploit them to your advantage. 10 x 7, soft cover, photos, illustrations, 194 pages.

CONTEMPORARY FIGHTING ARTS, LLC
"Real World Self Defense Since 1989"
www.sammyfranco.com
301-279-2244